CO...
LONDON
M25
jambuster™
GUIDE

ANTI-CLOCKWISE

CONTENTS

Hold-up between Junctions:

First published by Give Way Ltd 1997
This revised edition published by Collins 1998
An *imprint of* HarperCollins*Publishers*
77-85 Fulham Palace Road, Hammersmith, London W6 8JB

Mapping pages 2 to 32 © Give Way Ltd, 1998
Mapping pages 33 © Bartholomew 1998

Jambuster™ Guides are designed and researched by Give Way Ltd, Newcastle upon Tyne.
Project Director - Neil Atkinson. Senior Designer - Matthew Cook.

Jambuster™ is a trademark of HarperCollins*Publishers*.

Printed in Great Britain

ISBN 0 0044 8846 6   LC9983 MNA

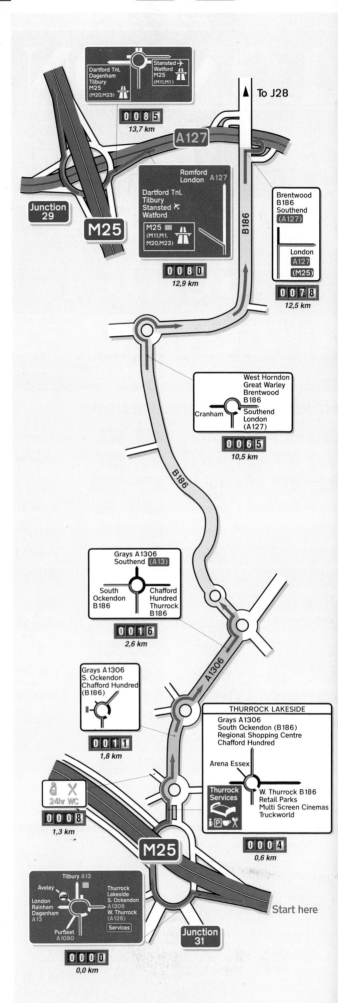

NOT TO SCALE

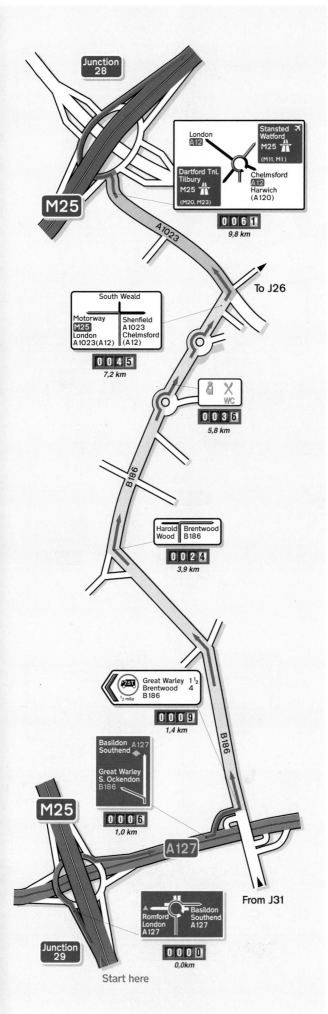

Junction 28

M25

London A12

Stansted Watford M25 (M11, M1)

Dartford Tnl Tilbury M25 (M20, M23)

Chelmsford A12 Harwich (A120)

0061
9,8 km

A1023

To J26

South Weald

Motorway M25 London A1023(A12)

Shenfield A1023 Chelmsford (A12)

0045
7,2 km

WC

0036
5,8 km

B186

Harold Wood | Brentwood B186

0024
3,9 km

7.5T Great Warley 1 ½ Brentwood 4 B186 ½ mile

0009
1,4 km

B186

Basildon Southend A127

Great Warley S. Ockendon B186

0006
1,0 km

M25

A127

From J31

Romford London A127

Basildon Southend A127

0000
0,0km

Junction 29

Start here

NOT TO SCALE

HGV WARNING! 7.5T

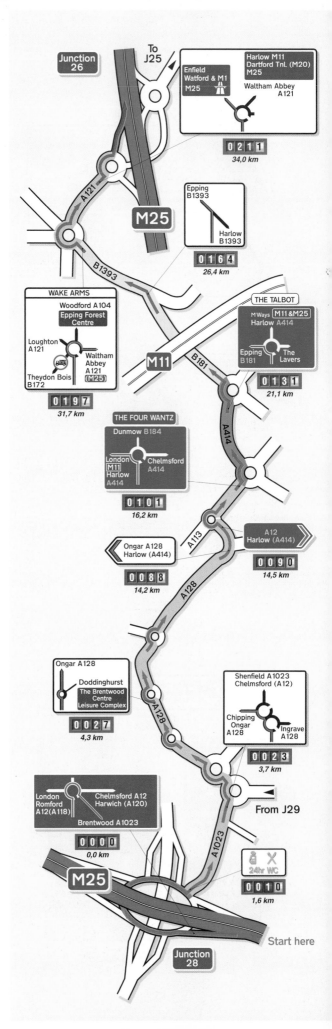

Junction 26

To J25

Enfield
Watford & M1
M25

Harlow M11
Dartford Tnl. (M20)
M25

Waltham Abbey
A121

`0 2 1 1`
34,0 km

M25

A121

Epping
B1393

Harlow
B1393

`0 1 6 4`
26,4 km

B1393

WAKE ARMS

Woodford A104
Epping Forest
Centre

Loughton
A121

Waltham
Abbey
A121
(M25)

Theydon Bois
B172

`0 1 9 7`
31,7 km

M11

THE TALBOT

M'Ways M11 & M25
Harlow A414

Epping
B181

The
Lavers

B181

`0 1 3 1`
21,1 km

A414

THE FOUR WANTZ

Dunmow B184

London
M11
Harlow
A414

Chelmsford
A414

`0 1 0 1`
16,2 km

A113

A12
Harlow (A414)

`0 0 9 0`
14,5 km

Ongar A128
Harlow (A414)

`0 0 8 8`
14,2 km

A128

Ongar A128

Doddinghurst

The Brentwood
Centre
Leisure Complex

`0 0 2 7`
4,3 km

A128

Shenfield A1023
Chelmsford (A12)

Chipping
Ongar
A128

Ingrave
A128

`0 0 2 3`
3,7 km

London
Romford
A12 (A118)

Chelmsford A12
Harwich (A120)

Brentwood A1023

`0 0 0 0`
0,0 km

From J29

A1023

24hr WC

`0 0 1 0`
1,6 km

M25

Start here

Junction 28

NOT TO SCALE

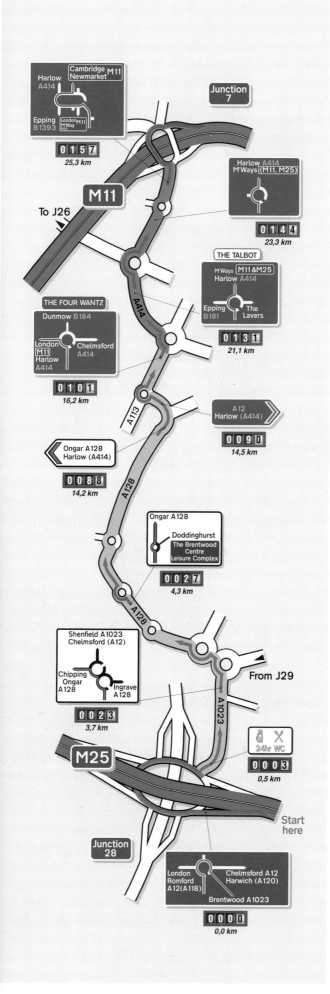

NOT TO SCALE

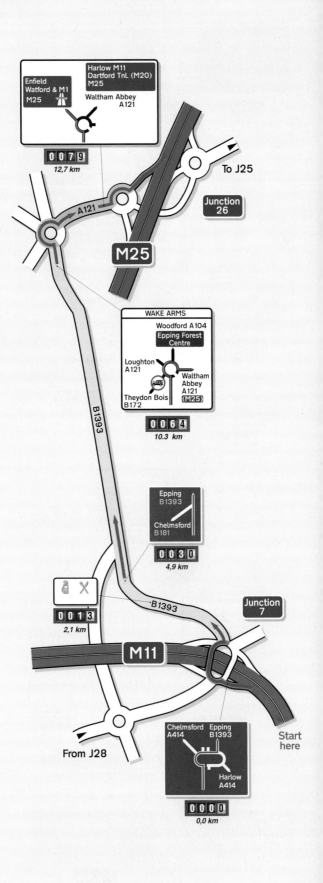

0079 12,7 km

Enfield
Watford & M1
M25

Harlow M11
Dartford TnL (M20)
M25
Waltham Abbey
A121

A121

To J25

Junction 26

M25

WAKE ARMS
Woodford A104
Epping Forest Centre
Loughton A121
Waltham Abbey A121 (M25)
Theydon Bois B172

0064 10.3 km

B1393

Epping B1393
Chelmsford B181

0030 4,9 km

B1393

Junction 7

0013 2,1 km

M11

From J28

Chelmsford A414   Epping B1393
Harlow A414

Start here

0000 0,0 km

NOT TO SCALE

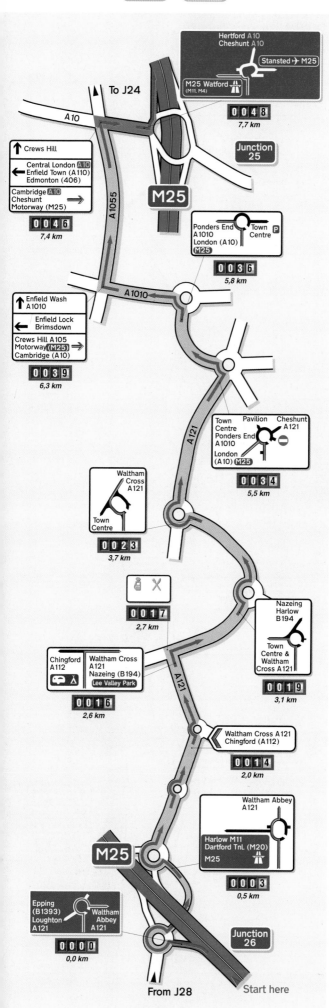

Hertford A10
Cheshunt A10
Stansted → M25
M25 Watford
(M11, M4)

0 0 4 8
7,7 km

To J24

A10

Junction 25

Crews Hill

Central London A10
Enfield Town (A110)
Edmonton (406)

Cambridge A10
Cheshunt
Motorway (M25)

0 0 4 6
7,4 km

A1055

M25

Ponders End
A1010
London (A10)
M25

Town Centre
P

0 0 3 6
5,8 km

A1010

Enfield Wash
A1010

Enfield Lock
Brimsdown

Crews Hill A105
Motorway (M25)
Cambridge (A10)

0 0 3 9
6,3 km

A121

Town
Centre
Ponders End
A1010
London
(A10) M25

Pavilion   Cheshunt
A121

0 0 3 4
5,5 km

Waltham
Cross
A121

Town
Centre

0 0 2 3
3,7 km

0 0 1 7
2,7 km

Nazeing
Harlow
B194

Town
Centre &
Waltham
Cross A121

0 0 1 9
3,1 km

A121

Chingford
A112

Waltham Cross
A121
Nazeing (B194)
Lee Valley Park

0 0 1 6
2,6 km

A121

Waltham Cross A121
Chingford (A112)

0 0 1 4
2,0 km

M25

Waltham Abbey
A121

Harlow M11
Dartford Tnl. (M20)
M25

0 0 0 3
0,5 km

Epping
(B1393)
Loughton
A121

Waltham
Abbey
A121

0 0 0 0
0,0 km

Junction 26

From J28

Start here

NOT TO SCALE

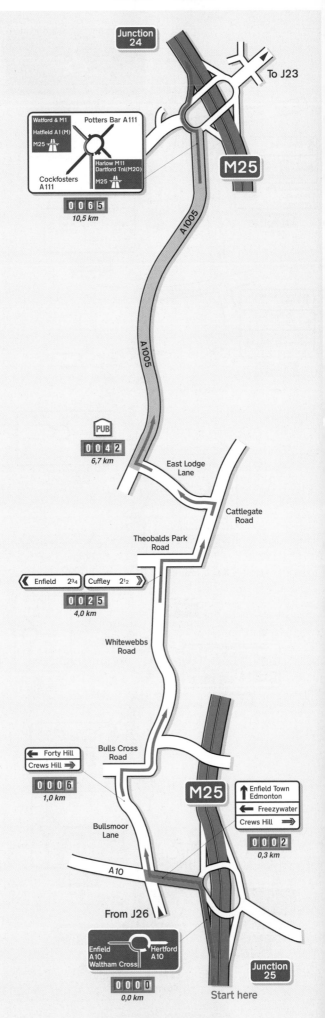

Junction 24

Watford & M1
Hatfield A1(M)
M25
Potters Bar A111
Harlow M11
Dartford Tnl(M20)
M25
Cockfosters A111

M25

`0 0 6 5`
10,5 km

A1005

A1005

PUB

`0 0 4 2`
6,7 km

East Lodge Lane

Cattlegate Road

Theobalds Park Road

Enfield 2³⁴ Cuffley 2¹²

`0 0 2 5`
4,0 km

Whitewebbs Road

Bulls Cross Road

Forty Hill
Crews Hill

`0 0 0 6`
1,0 km

M25

Enfield Town Edmonton
Freezywater
Crews Hill

`0 0 0 2`
0,3 km

Bullsmoor Lane

A10

From J26

Enfield A10
Waltham Cross
Hertford A10

`0 0 0 0`
0,0 km

Start here

Junction 25

NOT TO SCALE

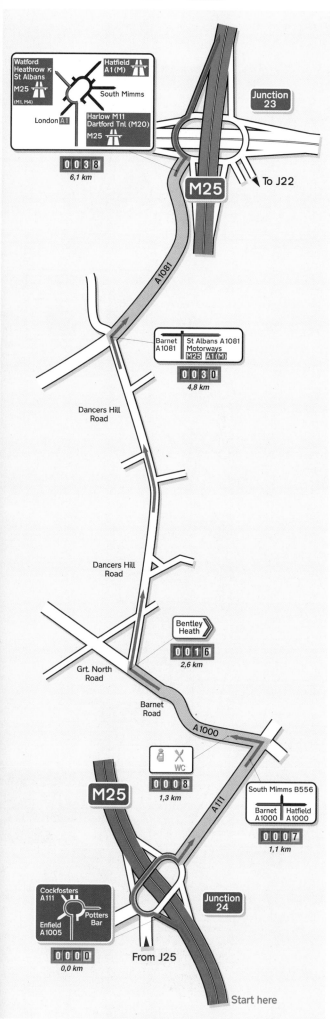

Watford
Heathrow ✈
St Albans
M25 🛣
(M1, M4)

Hatfield
A1(M) 🛣

South Mimms

London A1

Harlow M11
Dartford Tnl (M20)
M25 🛣

0 0 3 8
6,1 km

Junction
23

M25

To J22

A1081

Barnet
A1081

St Albans A1081
Motorways
M25 A1(M)

0 0 3 0
4,8 km

Dancers Hill
Road

Dancers Hill
Road

Bentley
Heath

0 0 1 6
2,6 km

Grt. North
Road

Barnet
Road

A1000

🍴 ✗
WC

0 0 0 8
1,3 km

M25

A111

South Mimms B556

Barnet
A1000 | Hatfield
A1000

0 0 0 7
1,1 km

Cockfosters
A111

Potters
Bar

Enfield
A1005

0 0 0 0
0,0 km

Junction
24

From J25

Start here

NOT TO SCALE

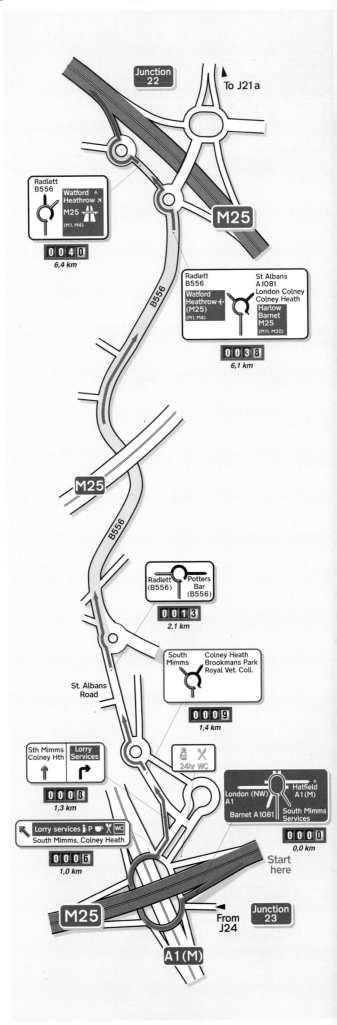

NOT TO SCALE

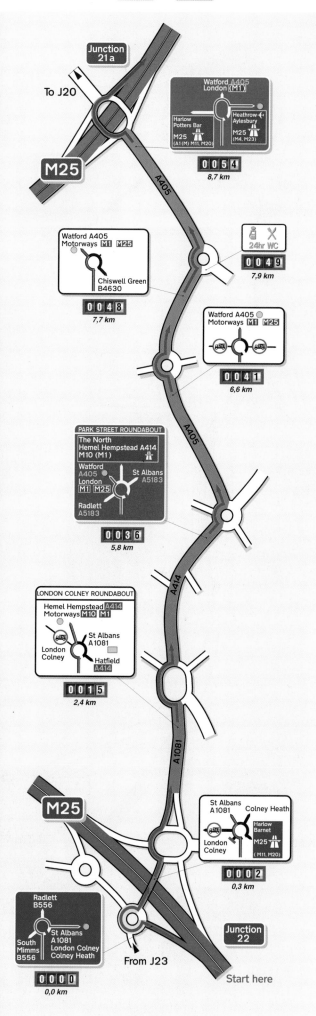

Junction 21a

To J20

M25

Watford A405
London (M1)
Harlow
Potters Bar
M25
(A1(M) M11, M20)
Heathrow
Aylesbury
M25
(M4, M23)
`0 0 5 4`
8,7 km

24hr WC
`0 0 4 9`
7,9 km

Watford A405
Motorways M1 M25
Chiswell Green
B4630
`0 0 4 8`
7,7 km

Watford A405
Motorways M1 M25
`0 0 4 1`
6,6 km

PARK STREET ROUNDABOUT
The North
Hemel Hempstead A414
M10 (M1)
Watford
A405
London
M1 M25
St Albans
A5183
Radlett
A5183
`0 0 3 6`
5,8 km

A405

A414

LONDON COLNEY ROUNDABOUT
Hemel Hempstead A414
Motorways M10 M1
St Albans
A1081
London
Colney
Hatfield
A414
`0 0 1 5`
2,4 km

A1081

M25

St Albans
A1081
Colney Heath
London
Colney
Harlow
Barnet
M25
(M11, M20)
`0 0 0 2`
0,3 km

Radlett
B556
South
Mimms
B556
St Albans
A1081
London Colney
Colney Heath
`0 0 0 0`
0,0 km

From J23

Junction 22

Start here

NOT TO SCALE

Hold-up between M25 Junc 21a M25 Junc 20 Anti-clockwise

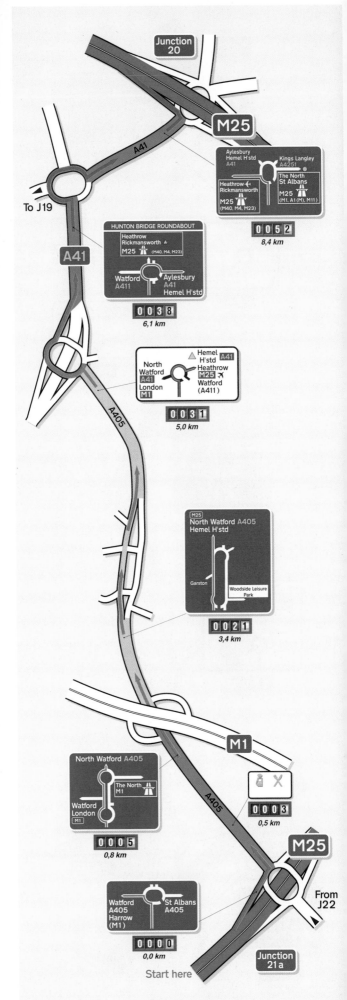

Junction 20
M25
Aylesbury
Hemel H'std
A41
Kings Langley
A4251
Heathrow
Rickmansworth
M25
(M40, M4, M23)
The North
St Albans
M25
(M1, A1(M), M11)
0052
8,4 km
A41
To J19
HUNTON BRIDGE ROUNDABOUT
Heathrow
Rickmansworth
M25 (M40, M4, M23)
Watford
A411
Aylesbury
A41
Hemel H'std
0038
6,1 km
A41
North
Watford
A41
London
M1
Hemel
H'std A41
Heathrow
M25
Watford
(A411)
0031
5,0 km
A405
M25
North Watford A405
Hemel H'std
Garston
Woodside Leisure
Park
0021
3,4 km
M1
North Watford A405
The North
M1
Watford
London
M1
0005
0,8 km
A405
0003
0,5 km
M25
From
J22
Watford
A405
Harrow
(M1)
St Albans
A405
0000
0,0 km
Junction
21a
Start here

NOT TO SCALE

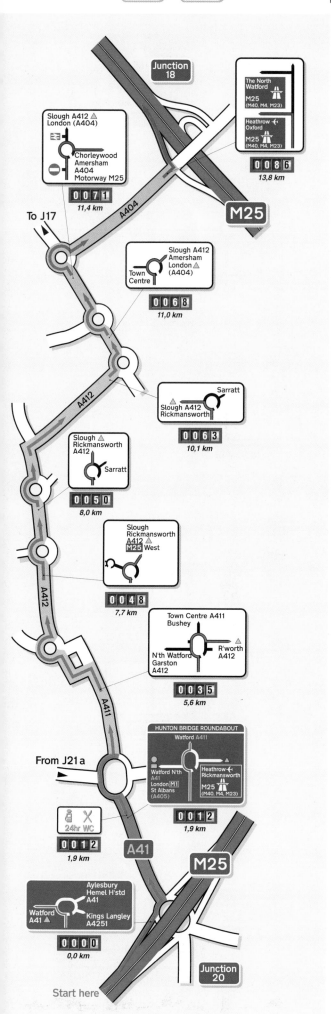

Junction 18

The North
Watford
M25
(M40, M4, M23)

Heathrow
Oxford
M25
(M40, M4, M23)

`0 0 8 6`
13,8 km

Slough A412 △
London (A404)

Chorleywood
Amersham
A404
Motorway M25

`0 0 7 1`
11,4 km

To J17

M25

Slough A412
Amersham
London △
(A404)

Town
Centre

`0 0 6 8`
11,0 km

Sarratt

Slough A412 △
Rickmansworth

`0 0 6 3`
10,1 km

Slough △
Rickmansworth
A412

Sarratt

`0 0 5 0`
8,0 km

Slough
Rickmansworth
A412 △
M25 West

`0 0 4 8`
7,7 km

Town Centre A411
Bushey

N'th Watford
Garston
A412

R'worth
A412

`0 0 3 5`
5,6 km

HUNTON BRIDGE ROUNDABOUT
Watford A411

Watford N'th
A41
London **M1**
St Albans
(A405)

Heathrow
Rickmansworth
M25
(M40, M4, M23)

`0 0 1 2`
1,9 km

From J21a

24hr WC

`0 0 1 2`
1,9 km

A41

M25

Aylesbury
Hemel H'std
A41

Watford
A41 △

Kings Langley
A4251

`0 0 0 0`
0,0 km

Start here

Junction 20

NOT TO SCALE

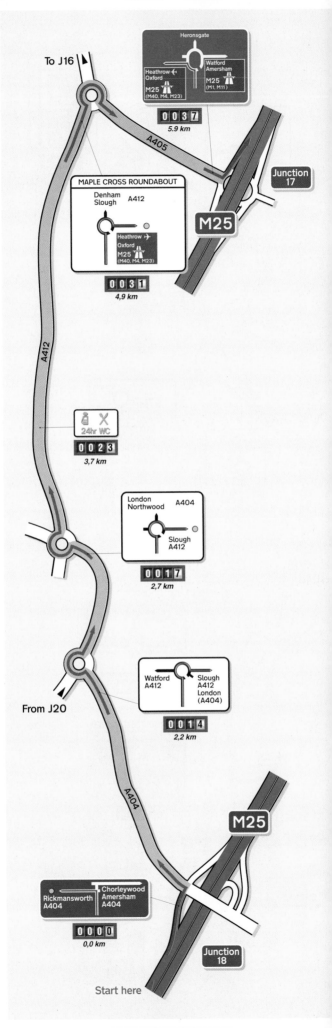

NOT TO SCALE

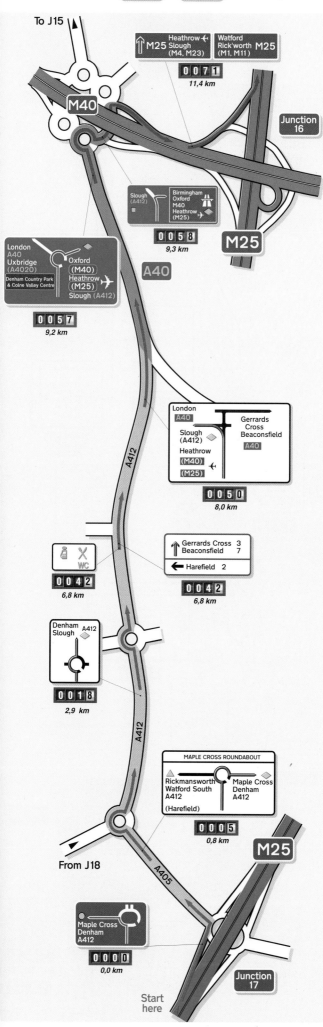

NOT TO SCALE

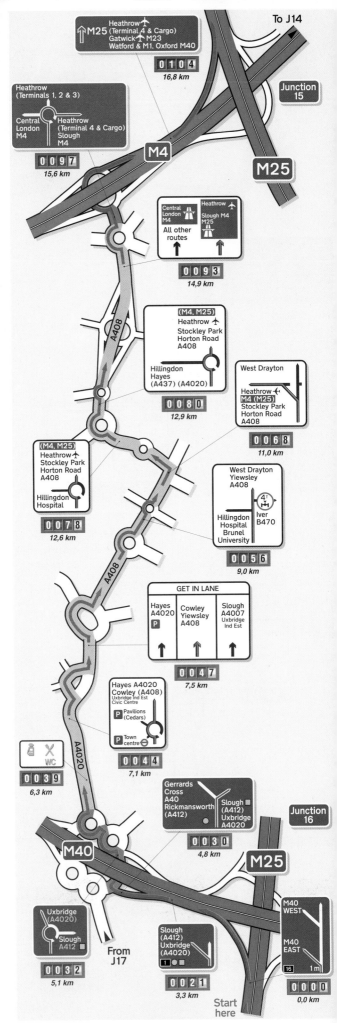

NOT TO SCALE

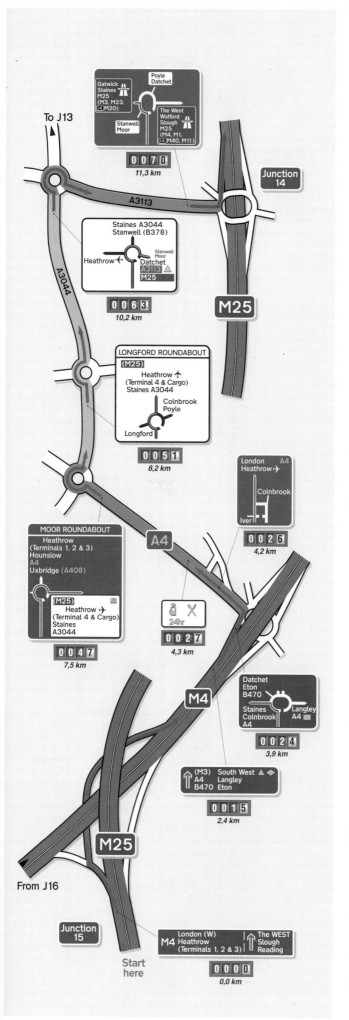

To J13

Gatwick
Staines
M25
(M3, M23,
14 M20)
Poyle
Datchet
Stanwell
Moor
The West
Watford
Slough
M25
(M4, M1,
14 M40, M11)

0 0 7 0
11,3 km

A3113

Junction
14

Staines A3044
Stanwell (B378)
Heathrow ✈
Stanwell
Moor
Datchet
A3113
M25

0 0 6 3
10,2 km

A3044

M25

LONGFORD ROUNDABOUT
(M25)
Heathrow ✈
(Terminal 4 & Cargo)
Staines A3044
Colnbrook
Poyle
Longford

0 0 5 1
8,2 km

London
Heathrow ✈
A4
Colnbrook
Iver

0 0 2 6
4,2 km

MOOR ROUNDABOUT
Heathrow
(Terminals 1, 2 & 3)
Hounslow
A4
Uxbridge (A408)
(M25)
Heathrow ✈
(Terminal 4 & Cargo)
Staines
A3044

0 0 4 7
7,5 km

A4

24hr

0 0 2 7
4,3 km

M4

Datchet
Eton
B470
Staines
Colnbrook
A4
Langley
A4

0 0 2 4
3,9 km

(M3)
A4
B470
South West
Langley
Eton

0 0 1 5
2,4 km

M25

From J16

Junction
15

Start
here

M4
London (W)
Heathrow
(Terminals 1, 2 & 3)
The WEST
Slough
Reading

0 0 0 0
0,0 km

NOT TO SCALE

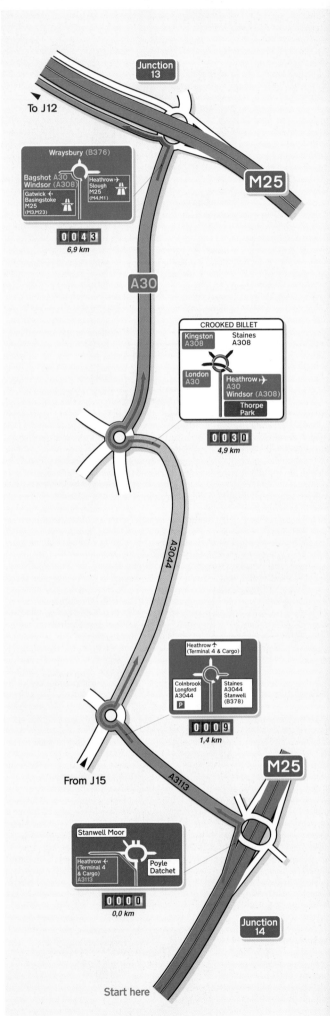

Junction 13

To J12

M25

Wraysbury (B376)

Bagshot A30
Windsor (A308)

Heathrow ✈
Slough
M25
(M4,M1)

Gatwick ←
Basingstoke
M25
(M3,M23)

`0 0 4 3`
6,9 km

A30

CROOKED BILLET

Kingston
A308

Staines
A308

London
A30

Heathrow ✈
A30
Windsor (A308)

Thorpe
Park

`0 0 3 0`
4,9 km

A3044

Heathrow ✈
(Terminal 4 & Cargo)

Colnbrook
Longford
A3044
P

Staines
A3044
Stanwell
(B378)

`0 0 0 9`
1,4 km

From J15

A3113

M25

Stanwell Moor

Heathrow ←
(Terminal 4
& Cargo)
A3113

Poyle
Datchet

`0 0 0 0`
0,0 km

Junction 14

Start here

NOT TO SCALE

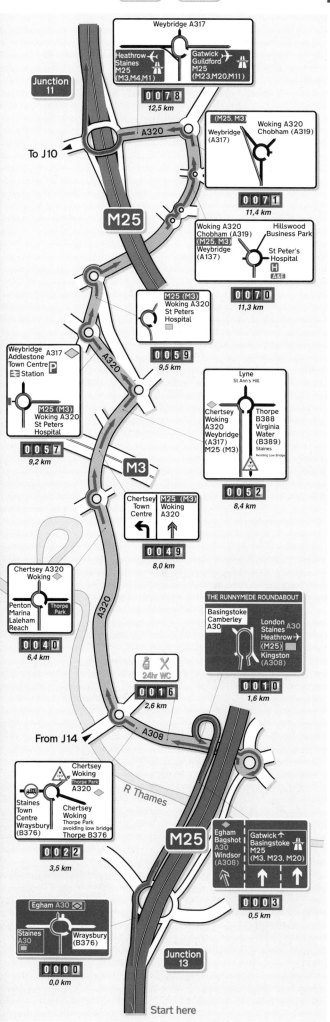

Junction 11

Weybridge A317

Heathrow Staines M25 (M3,M4,M1)

Gatwick Guildford M25 (M23,M20,M11)

0 0 7 8
12,5 km

(M25, M3) Weybridge (A317)

Woking A320 Chobham (A319)

0 0 7 1
11,4 km

To J10

M25

A320

Woking A320 Chobham (A319) (M25, M3) Weybridge (A137)

Hillswood Business Park

St Peter's Hospital
H A&E

0 0 7 0
11,3 km

M25 (M3) Woking A320 St Peters Hospital

0 0 5 9
9,5 km

Weybridge Addlestone Town Centre P
Station
A317

M25 (M3) Woking A320 St Peters Hospital

0 0 5 7
9,2 km

A320

M3

Lyne
St Ann's Hill

Chertsey Woking A320 Weybridge (A317) M25 (M3)

Thorpe B388 Virginia Water (B389) Staines
Avoiding Low Bridge

0 0 5 2
8,4 km

Chertsey Town Centre

M25 (M3) Woking A320

0 0 4 9
8,0 km

Chertsey A320 Woking

Penton Marina Laleham Reach

Thorpe Park

0 0 4 0
6,4 km

A320

THE RUNNYMEDE ROUNDABOUT

Basingstoke Camberley A30

London Staines Heathrow (M25)
Kingston (A308)
A30

0 0 1 0
1,6 km

24hr WC

0 0 1 6
2,6 km

From J14

A308

Chertsey Woking
Thorpe Park A320

Staines Town Centre Wraysbury (B376)

Chertsey Woking Thorpe Park avoiding low bridge Thorpe B376

0 0 2 2
3,5 km

R Thames

M25

Egham Bagshot A30 Windsor (A308)

Gatwick Basingstoke M25 (M3, M23, M20)

0 0 0 3
0,5 km

Egham A30

Staines A30

Wraysbury (B376)

0 0 0 0
0,0 km

Junction 13

Start here

NOT TO SCALE

HGV WARNING! 13'3"

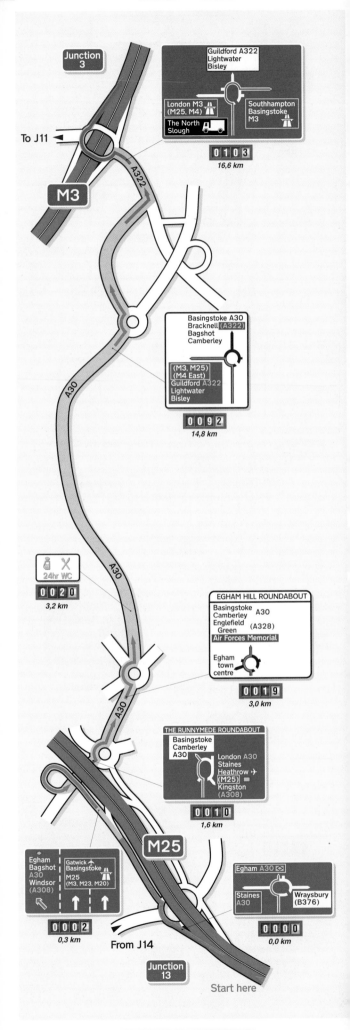

Junction 3

Guildford A322
Lightwater
Bisley

London M3
(M25, M4)
The North
Slough

Southhampton
Basingstoke
M3

To J11

M3

A322

`0 1 0 3`
16,6 km

Basingstoke A30
Bracknell (A322)
Bagshot
Camberley

(M3, M25)
(M4 East)
Guildford A322
Lightwater
Bisley

A30

`0 0 9 2`
14,8 km

24hr WC

A30

`0 0 2 0`
3,2 km

EGHAM HILL ROUNDABOUT

Basingstoke A30
Camberley
Englefield (A328)
Green
Air Forces Memorial

Egham
town
centre

A30

`0 0 1 9`
3,0 km

THE RUNNYMEDE ROUNDABOUT

Basingstoke
Camberley
A30

London A30
Staines
Heathrow ✈
(M25)
Kingston
(A308)

`0 0 1 0`
1,6 km

M25

Egham
Bagshot
A30
Windsor
(A308)

Gatwick
Basingstoke
M25
(M3, M23, M20)

Egham A30

Staines
A30

Wraysbury
(B376)

`0 0 0 2`
0,3 km

`0 0 0 0`
0,0 km

From J14

Junction 13

Start here

NOT TO SCALE

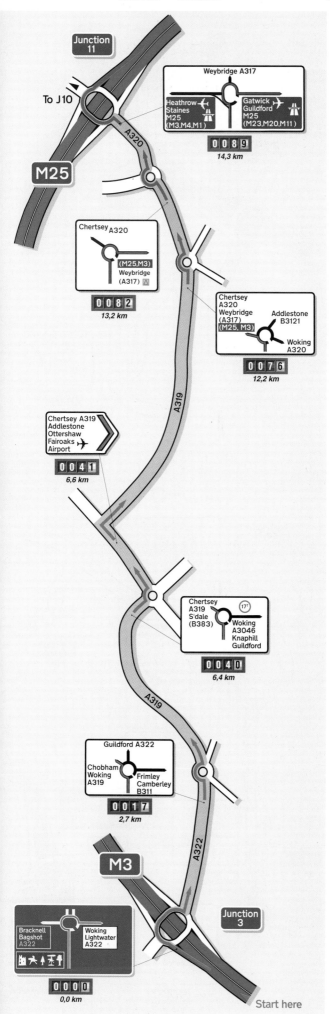

NOT TO SCALE

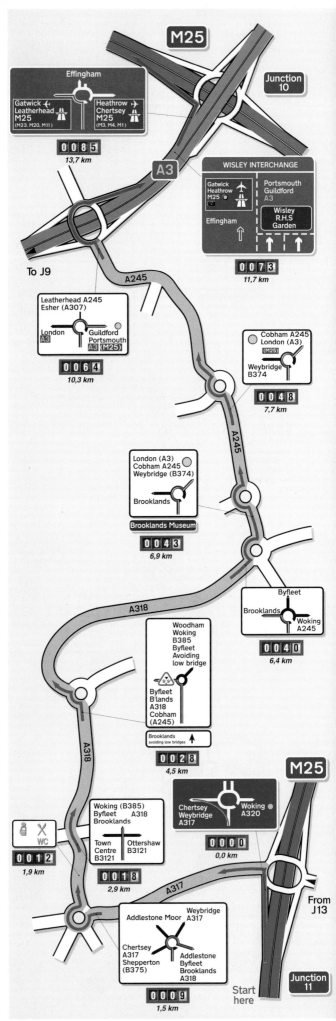

M25

Junction 10

Effingham

Gatwick Leatherhead M25 (M23, M20, M11)
Heathrow Chertsey M25 (M3, M4, M1)

0 0 8 5
13,7 km

A3

WISLEY INTERCHANGE

Gatwick Heathrow M25
Portsmouth Guildford A3
Wisley R.H.S Garden
Effingham

0 0 7 3
11,7 km

To J9

A245

Leatherhead A245 Esher (A307)
London A3
Guildford Portsmouth A3 (M25)

0 0 6 4
10,3 km

Cobham A245 London (A3) (M25)
Weybridge B374

0 0 4 8
7,7 km

A245

London (A3) Cobham A245 Weybridge (B374)
Brooklands

Brooklands Museum

0 0 4 3
6,9 km

A318

Byfleet
Brooklands
Woking A245

0 0 4 0
6,4 km

Woodham Woking B385 Byfleet Avoiding low bridge

Byfleet B'lands A318 Cobham (A245)

Brooklands avoiding low bridges

0 0 2 8
4,5 km

A318

M25

Chertsey Weybridge A317
Woking A320

0 0 0 0
0,0 km

Woking (B385) Byfleet A318 Brooklands
Town Centre B3121
Ottershaw B3121

0 0 1 8
2,9 km

WC

0 0 1 2
1,9 km

A317

From J13

Addlestone Moor
Weybridge A317
Chertsey A317 Shepperton (B375)
Addlestone Byfleet Brooklands A318

0 0 0 9
1,5 km

Start here

Junction 11

HGV WARNING! 9'.9'

NOT TO SCALE

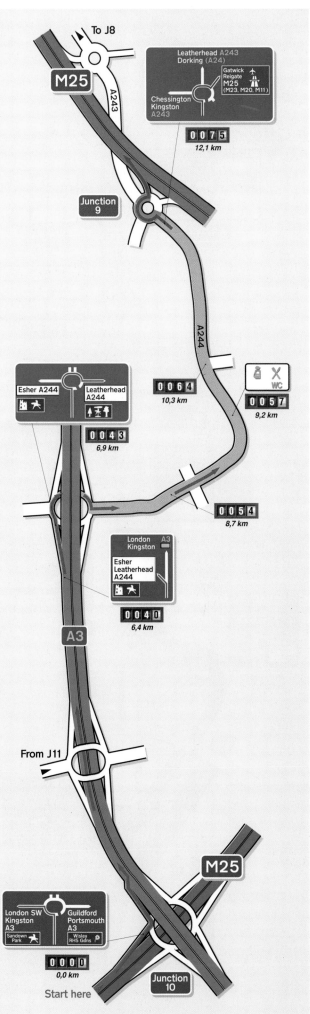

NOT TO SCALE

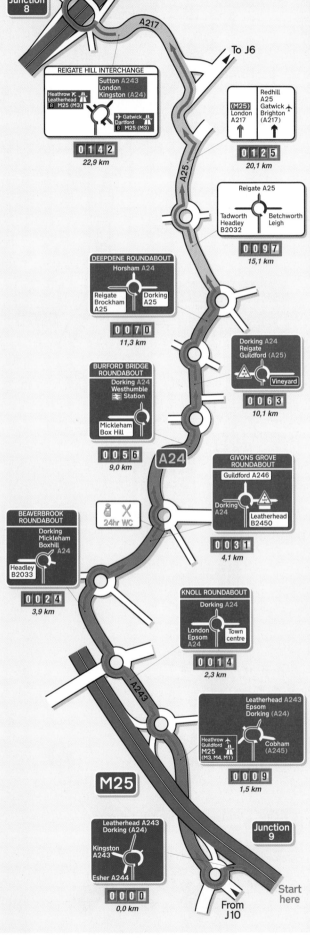

NOT TO SCALE

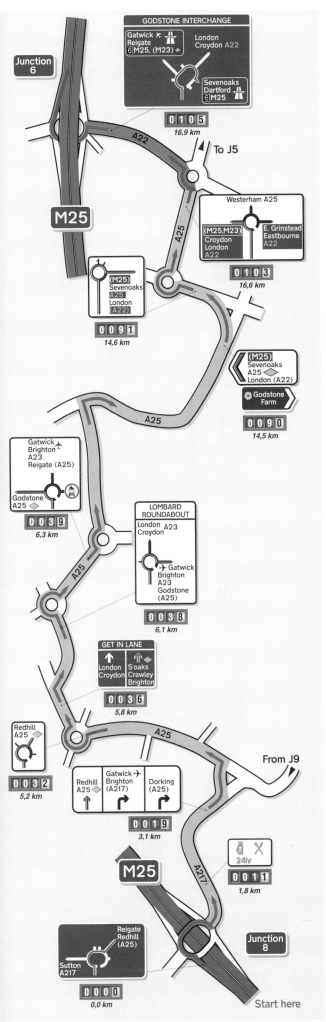

NOT TO SCALE

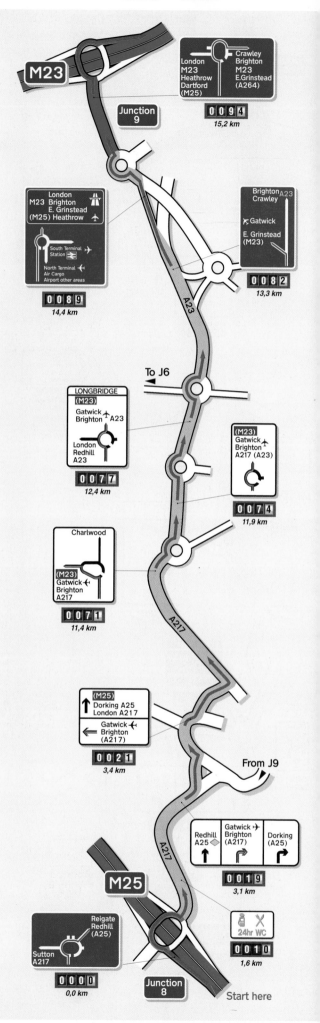

NOT TO SCALE

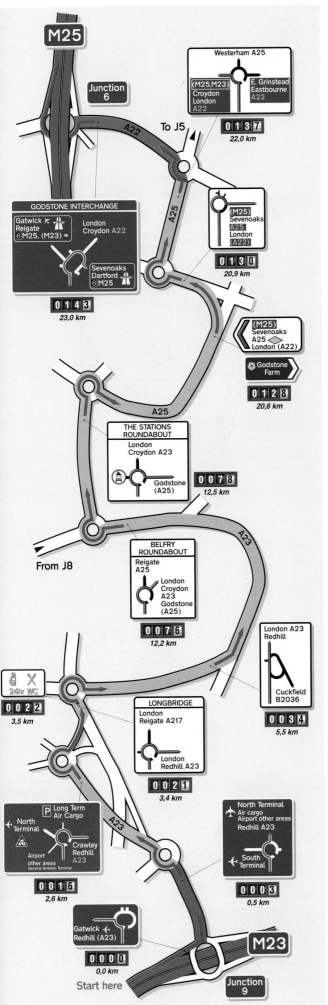

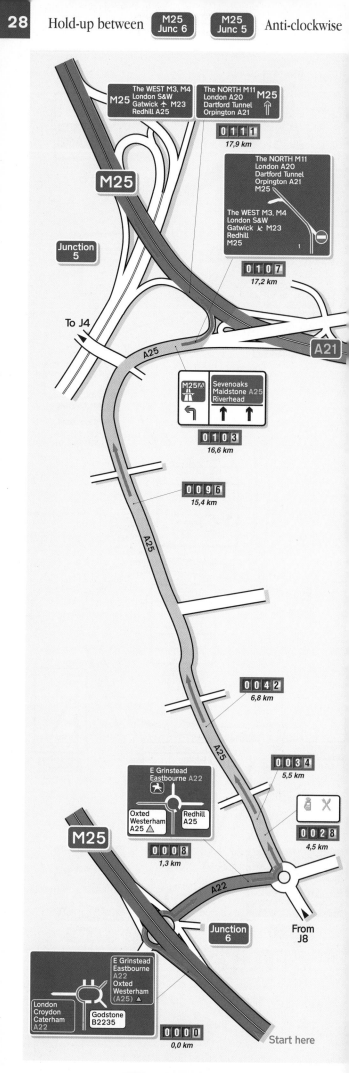

NOT TO SCALE

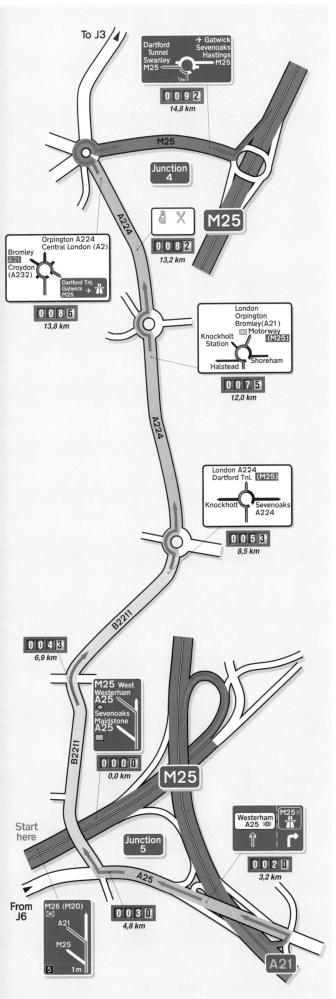

To J3

Dartford
Tunnel
Swanley
M25 → Gatwick
Sevenoaks
Hastings
M25
½m
[0 0 9 2]
14,8 km

M25

Junction
4

M25

[0 0 8 2]
13,2 km

Orpington A224
Central London (A2)
Bromley
A21
Croydon
(A232)
Dartford Tnl.
Gatwick
M25
[0 0 8 6]
13,8 km

London
Orpington
Bromley (A21)
Motorway
(M25)
Knockholt
Station
Halstead   Shoreham
[0 0 7 5]
12,0 km

A224

London A224
Dartford Tnl. (M25)
Knockholt   Sevenoaks
A224
[0 0 5 3]
8,5 km

B2211

[0 0 4 3]
6,9 km

M25 West
Westerham
A25
Sevenoaks
Maidstone
A25
[0 0 0 0]
0,0 km

M25

Westerham
A25
M25
[0 0 2 0]
3,2 km

B2211

Start
here

Junction
5

A25

From
J6

M26 (M20)
A21
M25
5   1m
[0 0 3 0]
4,8 km

A21

NOT TO SCALE

M25

Junction 3

To J2

Swanley A20
Motorways
(M25,M20)

Dartford
A225

0 0 6 9
11,7 km

A20

Swanley
B2173   London **A20**

Dartford
Tunnel
M25
(M1l,M1)

Gatwick ✈
Sevenoaks
The WEST
M25
(M23,M4)

Maidstone
Channel Tunnel
Dover
M20

0 0 8 2
13,2 km

24hr WC

0 0 7 1
11,4 km

A225

Swanley A20
Dartford (A225)
Motorways
(M25,M20)

W.Kingsdown
A20
(Via Roundabout)

0 0 6 5
10,5 km

CASTLE ROAD
0 0 5 5
8,8 km

Eynsford
Farningham
A225

Shoreham
Otford
A225

0 0 5 6
9,0 km

M25

CHURCH ROAD
0 0 1 5
2,4 km

↑ Chelsfield Station
Chelsfield Village ➡

0 0 1 4
2,3 km

Bromley
A21
Croydon
(A232)

Orpington
A224

Dunton
Green
A224

0 0 0 7
1,1 km

M25

A224

M25

From
J5

Junction 4

Bromley
A21
Orpington
A224

0 0 0 0
0,0 km

Start here

NOT TO SCALE

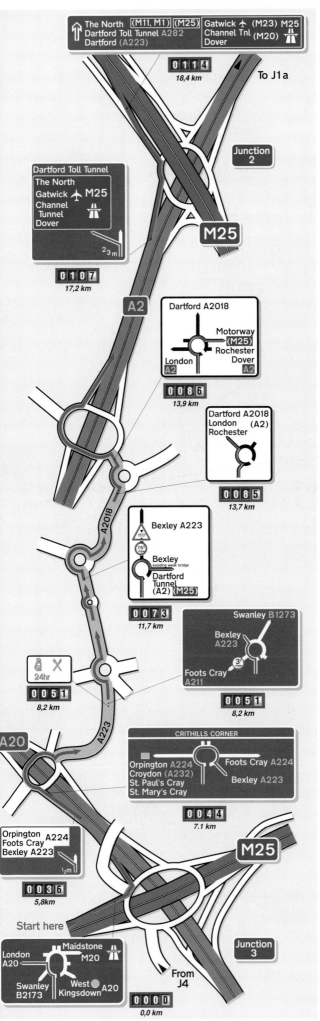

NOT TO SCALE

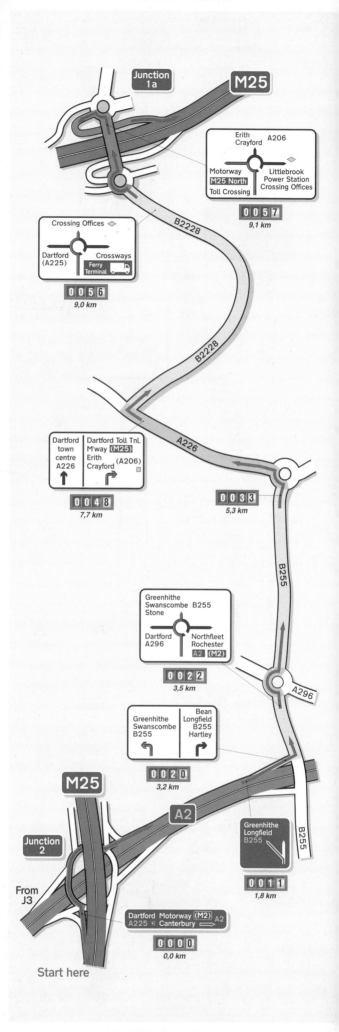

NOT TO SCALE

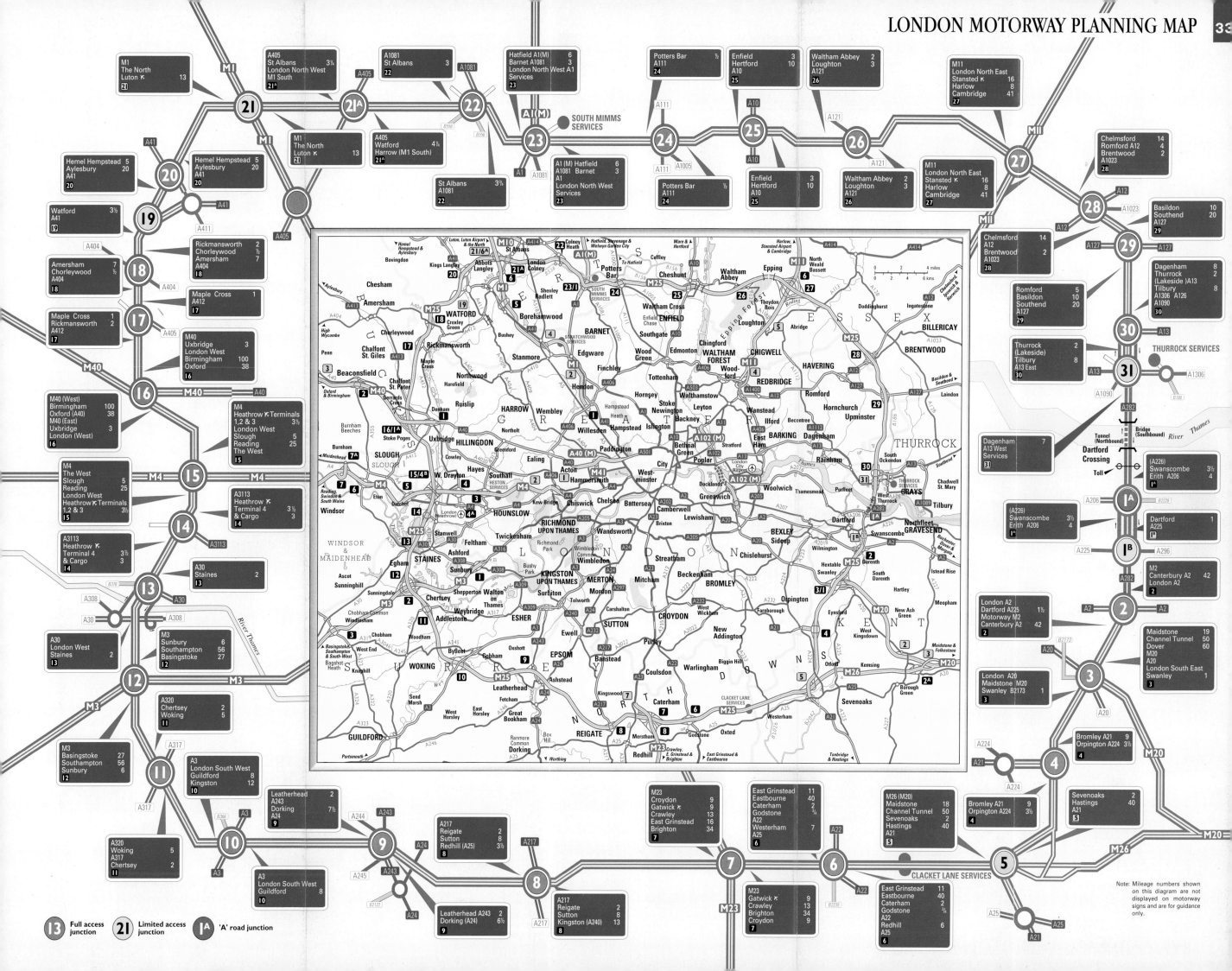

Legend:

13 Full access junction **21** Limited access junction **1ᴬ** 'A' road junction

Note: Mileage numbers shown on this diagram are not displayed on motorway signs and are for guidance only.

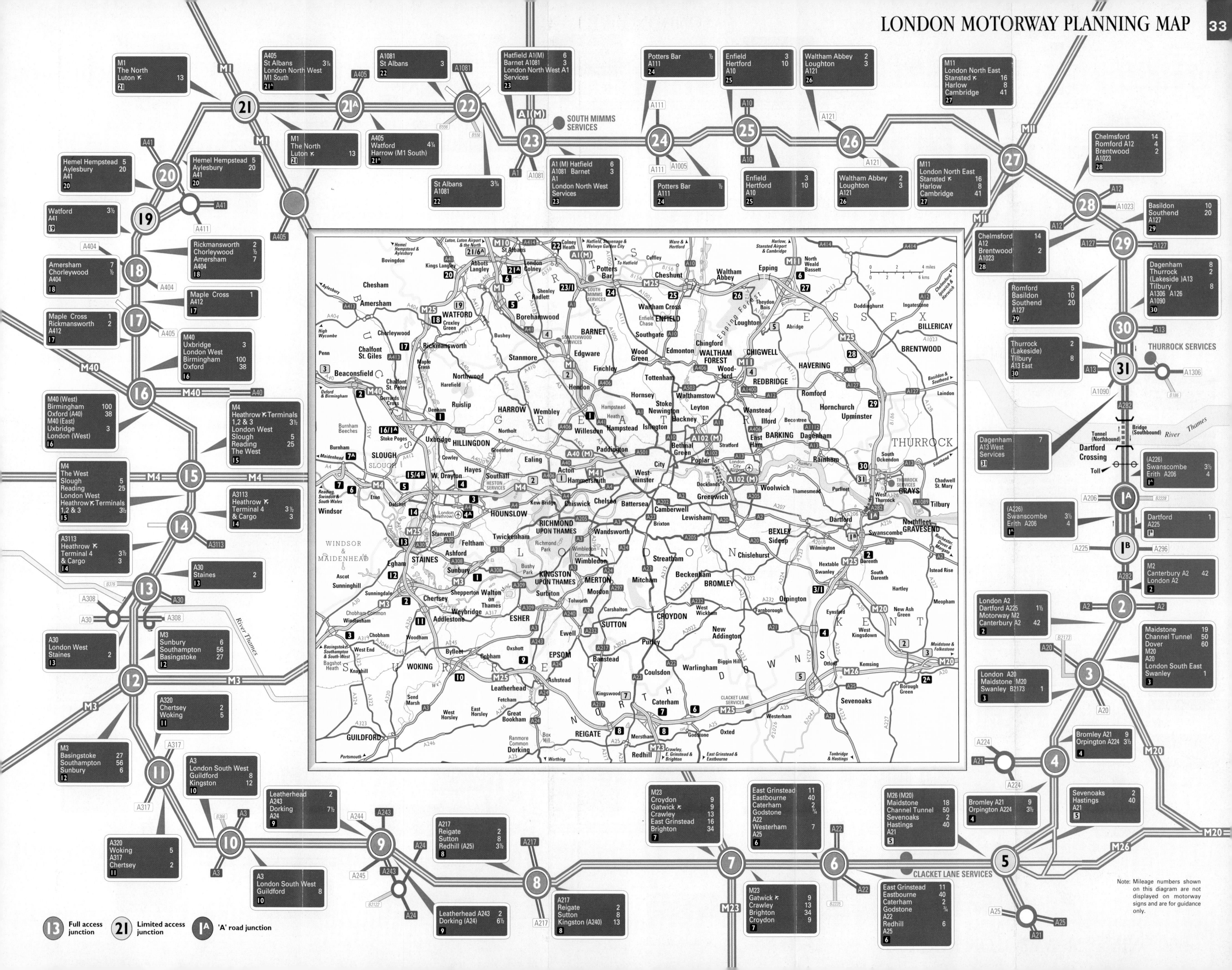

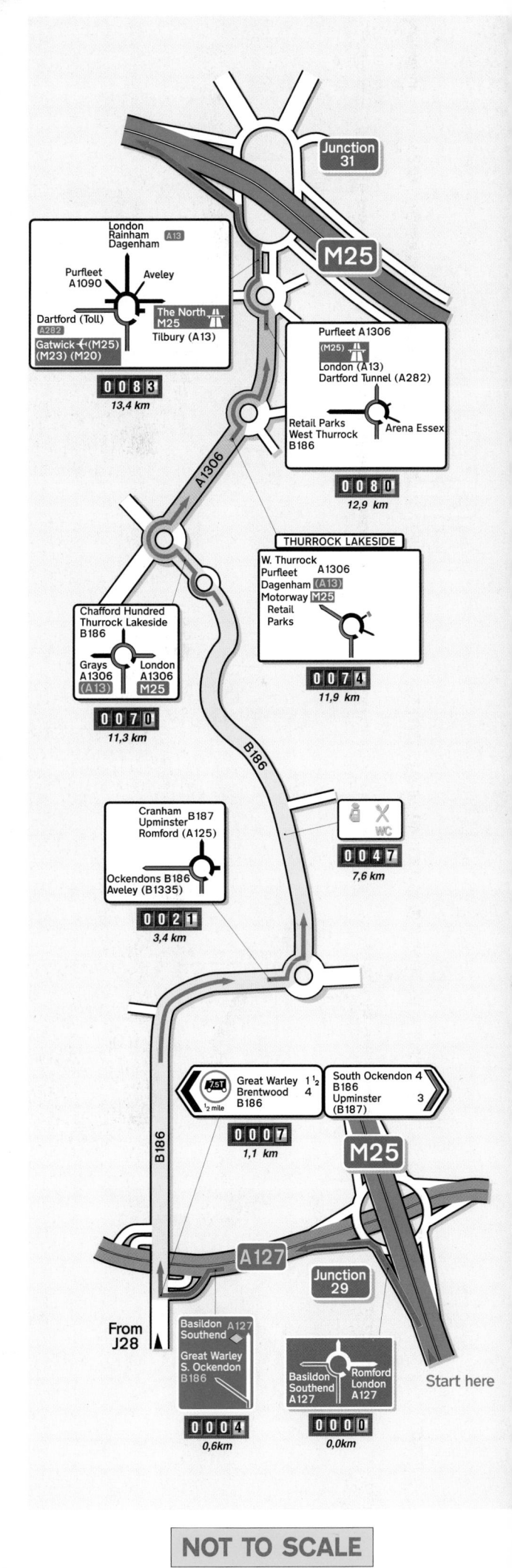

NOT TO SCALE

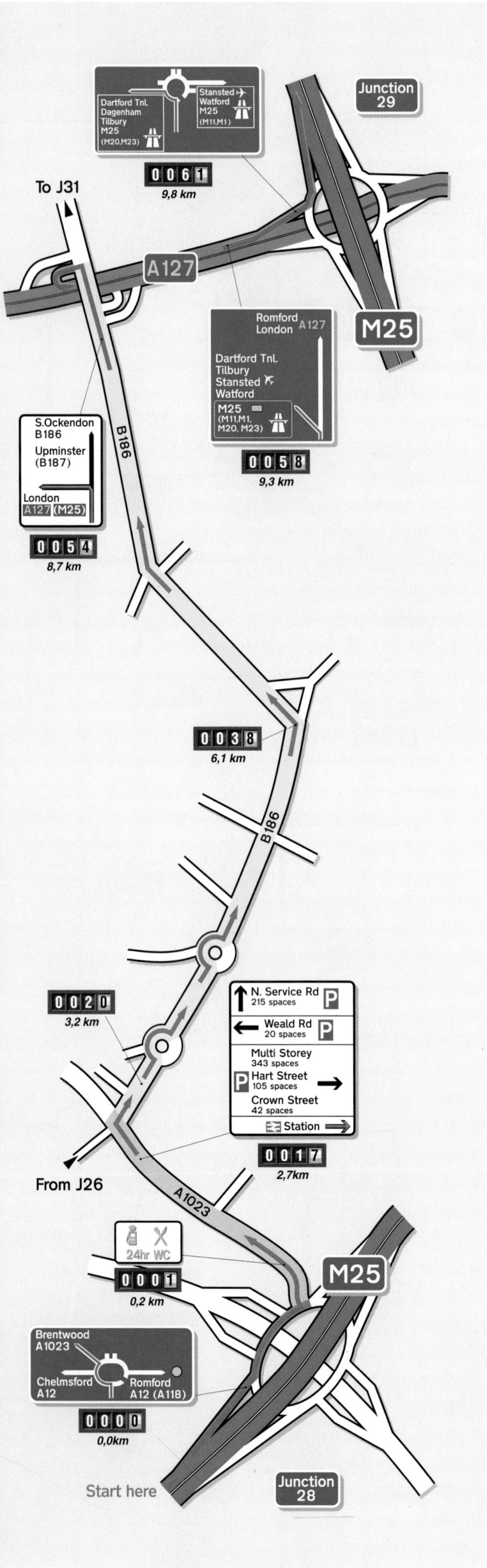

Junction 29

Dartford Tnl. Dagenham Tilbury M25 (M20,M23)

Stansted → Watford M25 (M11,M1)

0 0 6 1
9,8 km

To J31

A127

M25

Romford London A127

Dartford TnL Tilbury Stansted ✈ Watford M25 (M11,M1, M20, M23)

0 0 5 8
9,3 km

S.Ockendon B186

Upminster (B187)

London A127 (M25)

0 0 5 4
8,7 km

B186

0 0 3 8
6,1 km

B186

N. Service Rd
215 spaces P

← Weald Rd
20 spaces P

Multi Storey
343 spaces

P Hart Street
105 spaces →

Crown Street
42 spaces

Station ⟹

0 0 2 0
3,2 km

0 0 1 7
2,7km

From J26

A1023

24hr WC

0 0 0 1
0,2 km

M25

Brentwood A1023

Chelmsford A12   Romford A12 (A118)

0 0 0 0
0,0km

Start here

Junction 28

NOT TO SCALE

Hold-up between M11 Junc 7 M25 Junc 28 Clockwise

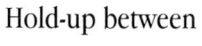

NOT TO SCALE

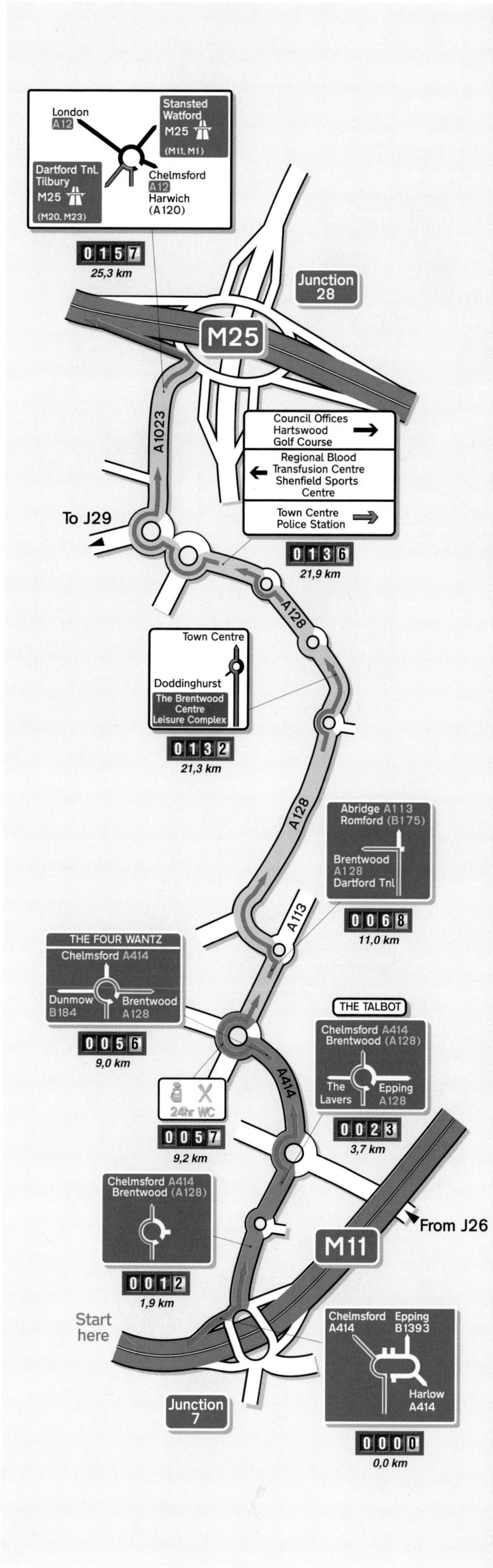

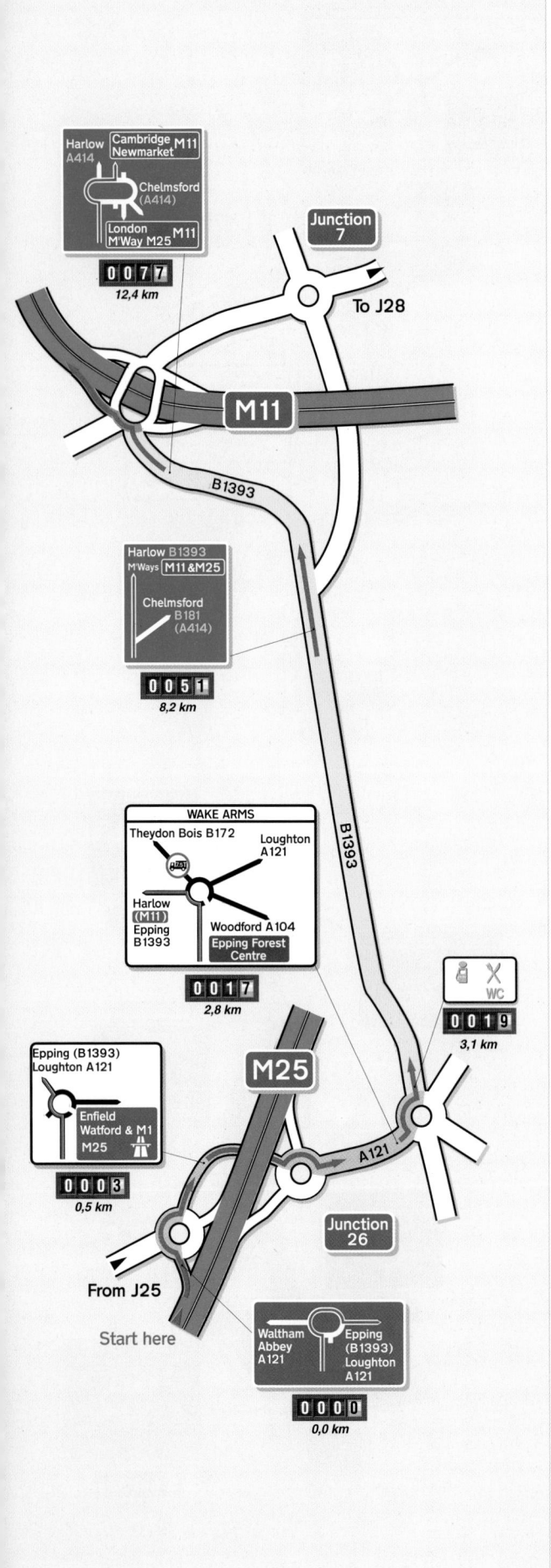

NOT TO SCALE

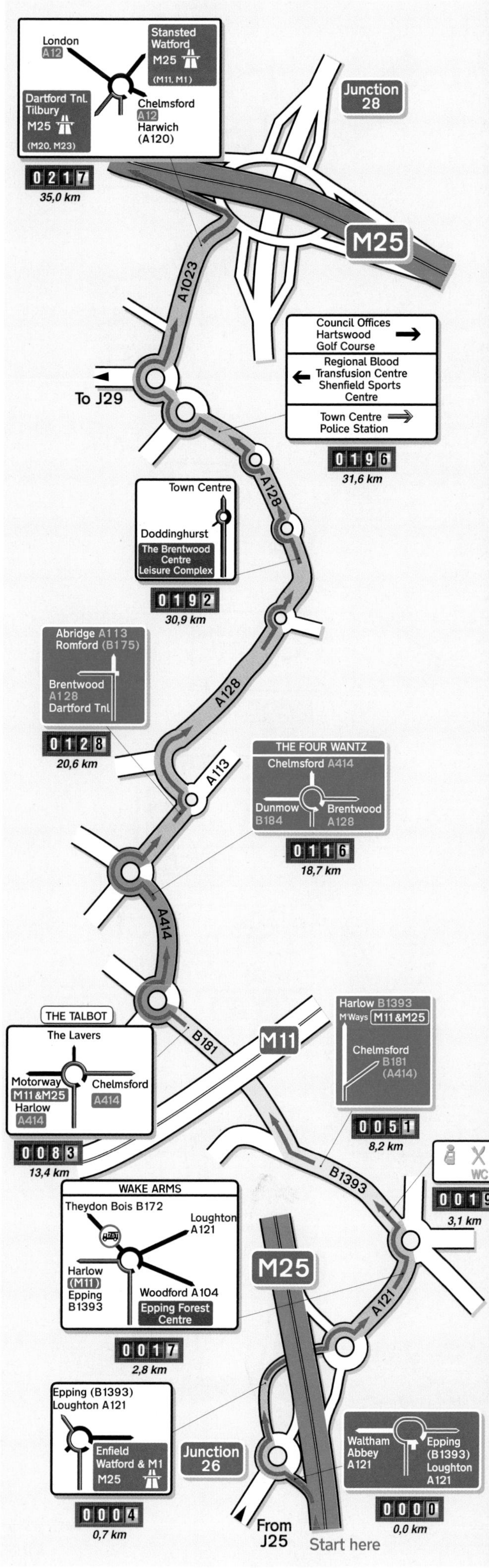

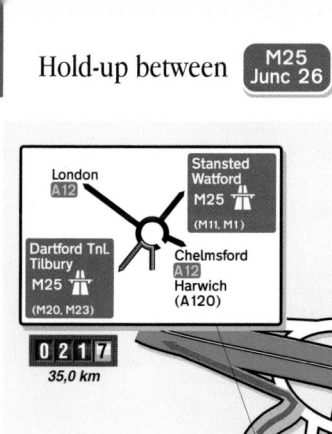

London A12
Stansted Watford M25 (M11, M1)
Dartford Tnl Tilbury M25 (M20, M23)
Chelmsford A12 Harwich (A120)

0 2 1 7
35,0 km

Junction 28

M25

Council Offices Hartswood Golf Course →
← Regional Blood Transfusion Centre Shenfield Sports Centre
Town Centre → Police Station

0 1 9 6
31,6 km

To J29

A1023

A128

Town Centre
Doddinghurst
The Brentwood Centre Leisure Complex

0 1 9 2
30,9 km

Abridge A113
Romford (B175)
Brentwood A128 Dartford Tnl

0 1 2 8
20,6 km

A128

A113

THE FOUR WANTZ
Chelmsford A414
Dunmow B184
Brentwood A128

0 1 1 6
18,7 km

A414

THE TALBOT
The Lavers
Motorway M11 & M25 Harlow A414
Chelmsford A414

0 0 8 3
13,4 km

B181

M11

Harlow B1393
M'Ways M11 & M25
Chelmsford B181 (A414)

0 0 5 1
8,2 km

B139.3

WC

0 0 1 9
3,1 km

WAKE ARMS
Theydon Bois B172
Loughton A121
Harlow (M11) Epping B1393
Woodford A104
Epping Forest Centre

M25

A121

0 0 1 7
2,8 km

Epping (B1393)
Loughton A121
Enfield Watford & M1 M25

Junction 26

Waltham Abbey A121
Epping (B1393) Loughton A121

0 0 0 4
0,7 km

0 0 0 0
0,0 km

From J25
Start here

NOT TO SCALE

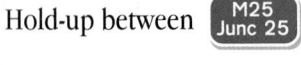

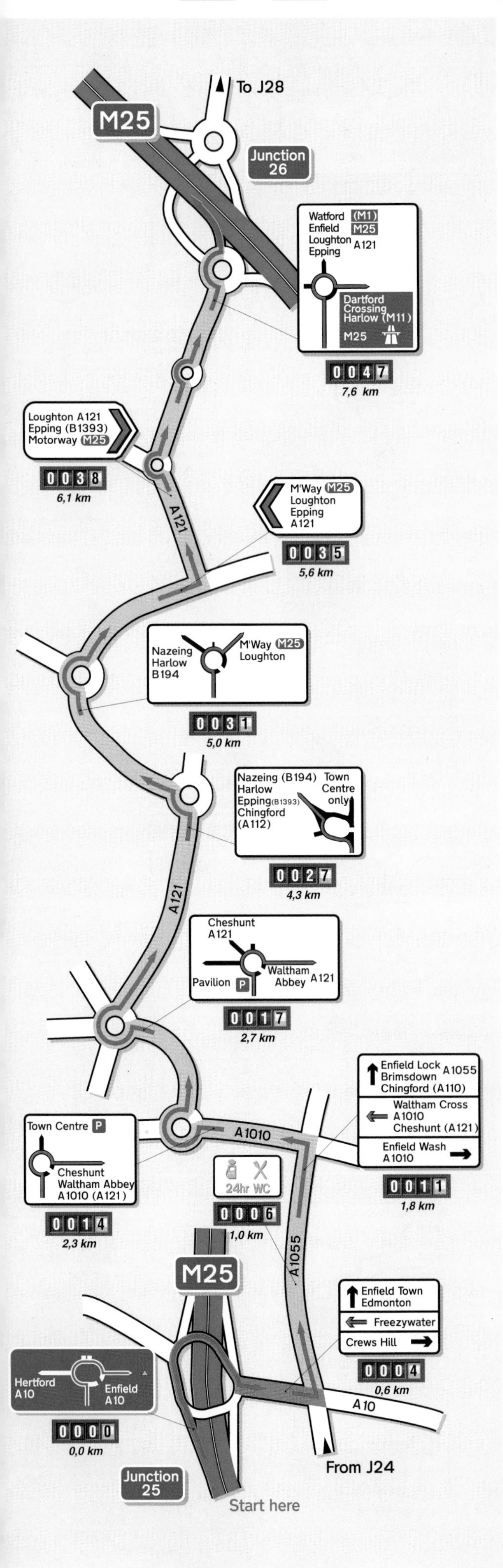

M25

To J28

Junction 26

Watford (M1)
Enfield (M25)
Loughton A121
Epping

Dartford
Crossing
Harlow (M11)
M25

0 0 4 7
7,6 km

Loughton A121
Epping (B1393)
Motorway (M25)

0 0 3 8
6,1 km

A121

M'Way (M25)
Loughton
Epping
A121

0 0 3 5
5,6 km

Nazeing
Harlow
B194

M'Way (M25)
Loughton

0 0 3 1
5,0 km

Nazeing (B194)   Town
Harlow   Centre
Epping (B1393)   only
Chingford
(A112)

0 0 2 7
4,3 km

A121

Cheshunt
A121

Pavilion P   Waltham
              Abbey A121

0 0 1 7
2,7 km

Enfield Lock A1055
Brimsdown
Chingford (A110)

Waltham Cross
A1010
Cheshunt (A121)

Enfield Wash
A1010

0 0 1 1
1,8 km

Town Centre P

A1010

Cheshunt
Waltham Abbey
A1010 (A121)

0 0 1 4
2,3 km

24hr WC

0 0 0 6
1,0 km

A1055

M25

Enfield Town
Edmonton

Freezywater

Crews Hill

0 0 0 4
0,6 km

Hertford   Enfield
A10   A10

A10

0 0 0 0
0,0 km

Junction 25

From J24

Start here

NOT TO SCALE

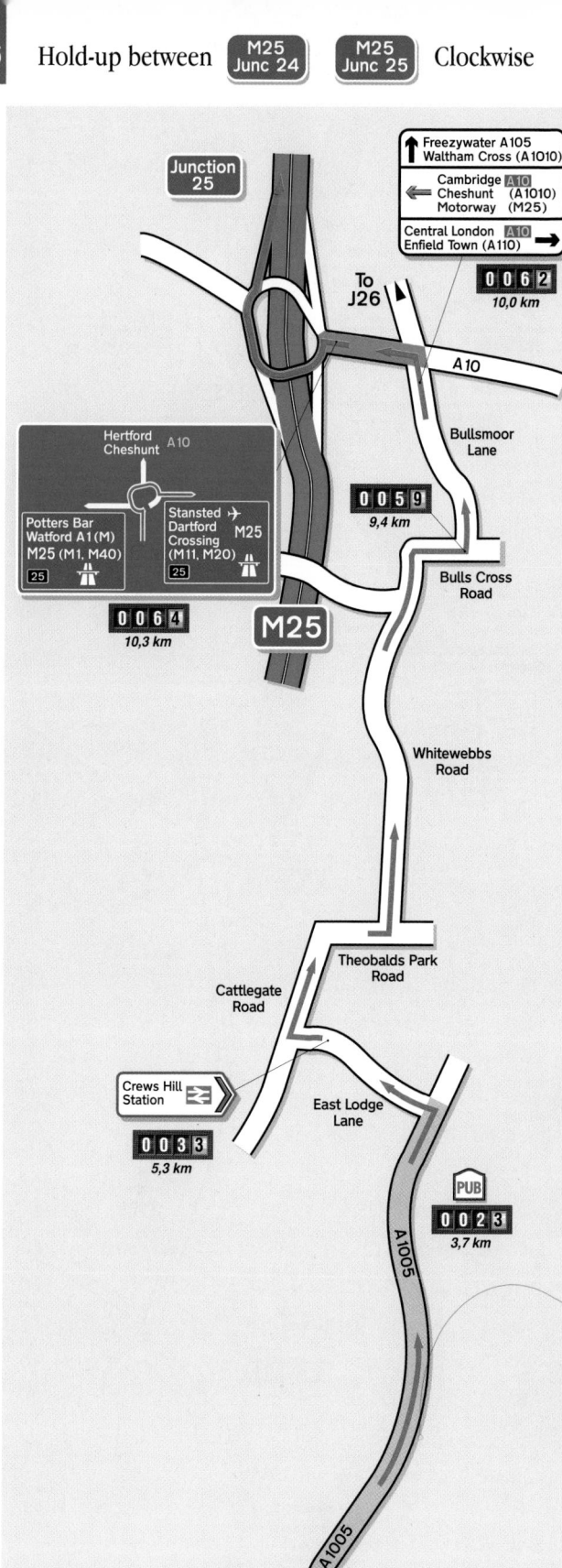

Junction 25

To J26

Freezywater A105
Waltham Cross (A1010)

↑ Cambridge A10
← Cheshunt (A1010)
Motorway (M25)

Central London A10
Enfield Town (A110) →

0062
10,0 km

A10

Bullsmoor Lane

Hertford A10
Cheshunt

Potters Bar
Watford A1(M)
M25 (M1, M40)
25 🛣

Stansted ✈
Dartford
Crossing
(M11, M20)
25 🛣 M25

0064
10,3 km

0059
9,4 km

Bulls Cross Road

M25

Whitewebbs Road

Cattlegate Road

Theobalds Park Road

Crews Hill Station 🚉

East Lodge Lane

0033
5,3 km

A1005

PUB
0023
3,7 km

A1005

M25

Junction 24

Enfield A1005

Potters Bar
A111

Cockfosters
A111

0000
0,0 km

From J23

Start here

NOT TO SCALE

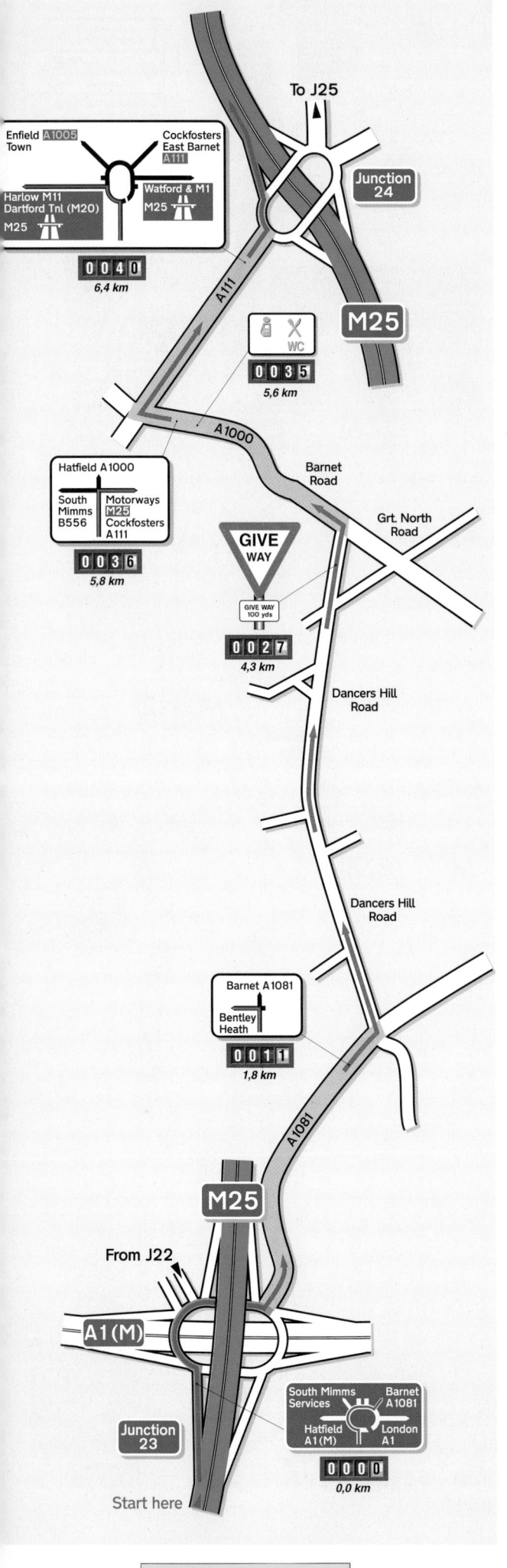

Enfield A1005 Town
Cockfosters East Barnet A111
Harlow M11 Dartford Tnl (M20) M25
Watford & M1 M25

`0 0 4 0`
6,4 km

To J25

Junction 24

M25

WC

`0 0 3 5`
5,6 km

A111

A1000

Hatfield A1000
South Mimms B556
Motorways M25 Cockfosters A111

`0 0 3 6`
5,8 km

Barnet Road

Grt. North Road

GIVE WAY

GIVE WAY 100 yds

`0 0 2 7`
4,3 km

Dancers Hill Road

Dancers Hill Road

Barnet A1081
Bentley Heath

`0 0 1 1`
1,8 km

A1081

M25

From J22

A1(M)

Junction 23

South Mimms Services
Barnet A1081
Hatfield A1(M)
London A1

`0 0 0 0`
0,0 km

Start here

NOT TO SCALE

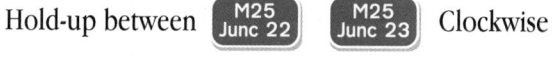

24 Hold-up between M25 Junc 22 M25 Junc 23 Clockwise

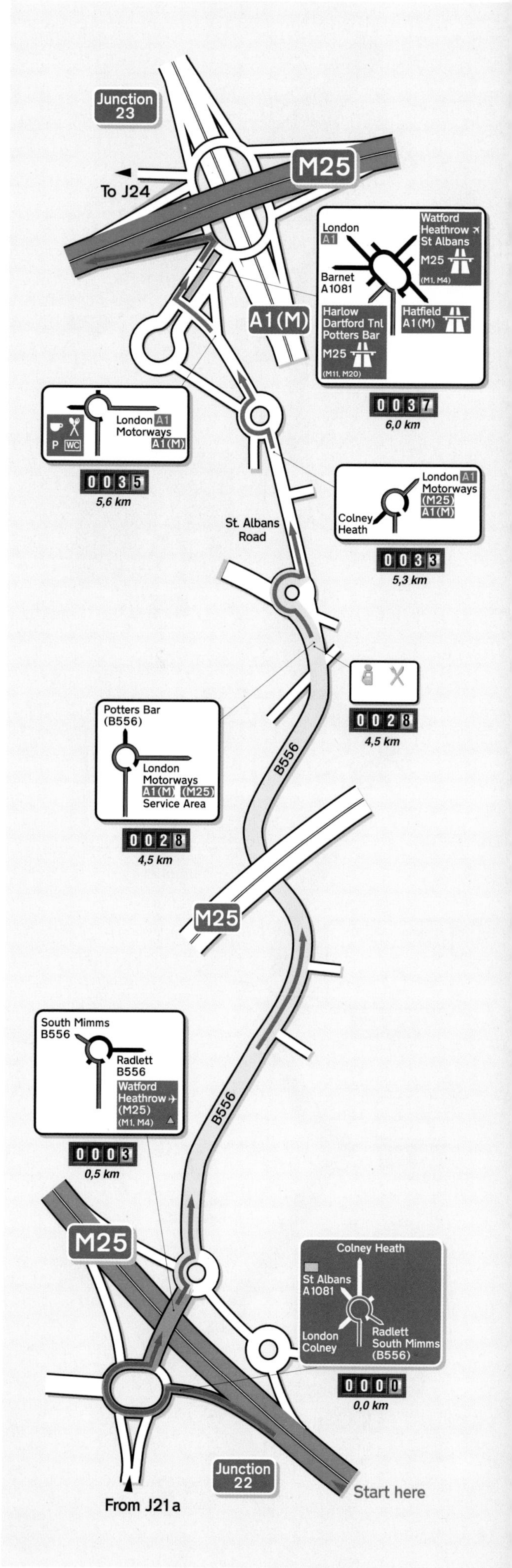
Junction 23
M25
To J24
London
A1
Watford
Heathrow
St Albans
M25
(M1, M4)
Barnet
A1081
Harlow
Dartford Tnl
Potters Bar
M25
(M11, M20)
Hatfield
A1(M)
A1(M)
0037
6,0 km
London A1
Motorways
A1(M)
P WC
0035
5,6 km
London A1
Motorways
(M25)
A1(M)
Colney Heath
0033
5,3 km
St. Albans Road
0028
4,5 km
Potters Bar
(B556)
London
Motorways
A1(M) (M25)
Service Area
0028
4,5 km
B556
M25
South Mimms
B556
Radlett
B556
Watford
Heathrow
(M25)
(M1, M4)
0003
0,5 km
B556
M25
Colney Heath
St Albans
A1081
London
Colney
Radlett
South Mimms
(B556)
0000
0,0 km
Junction 22
Start here
From J21a

NOT TO SCALE

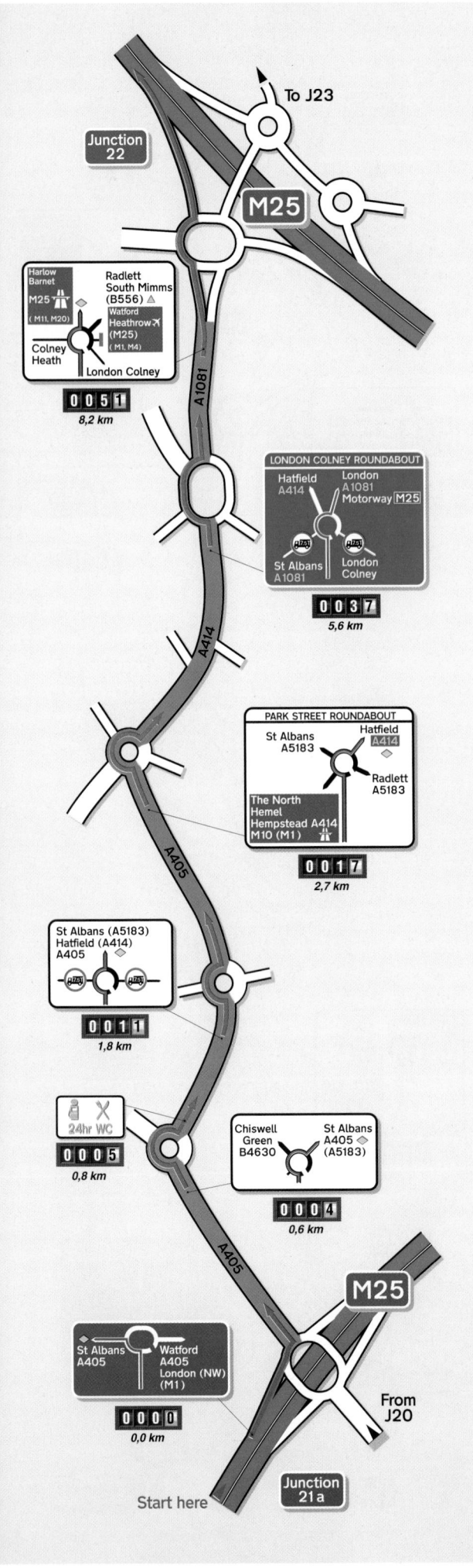

NOT TO SCALE

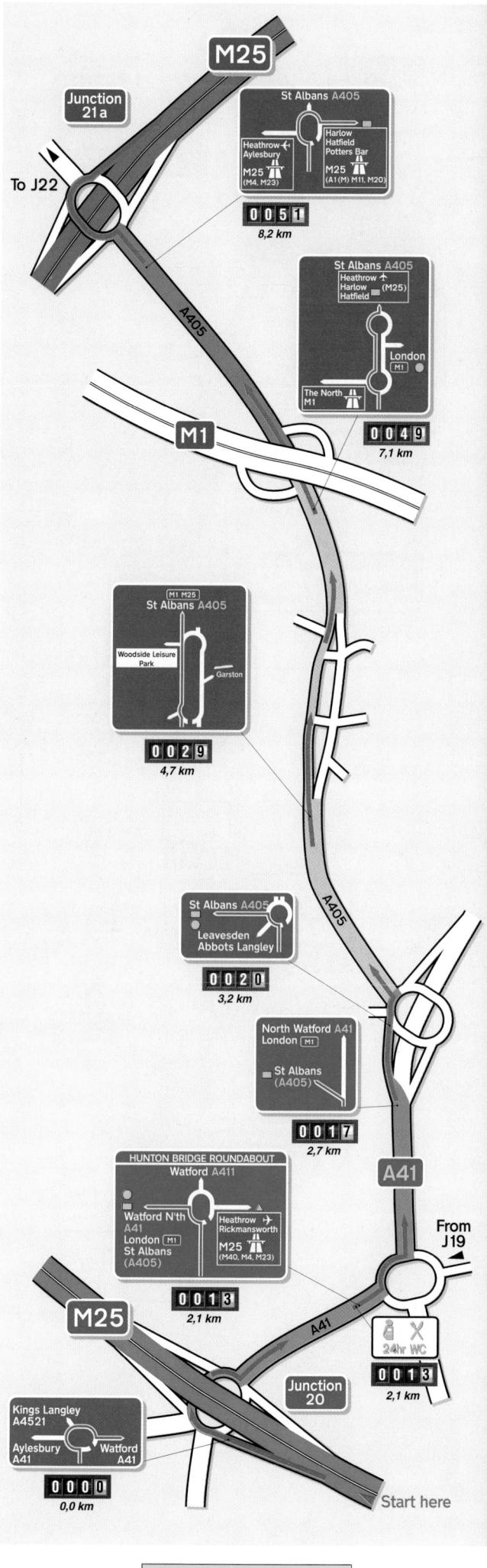

NOT TO SCALE

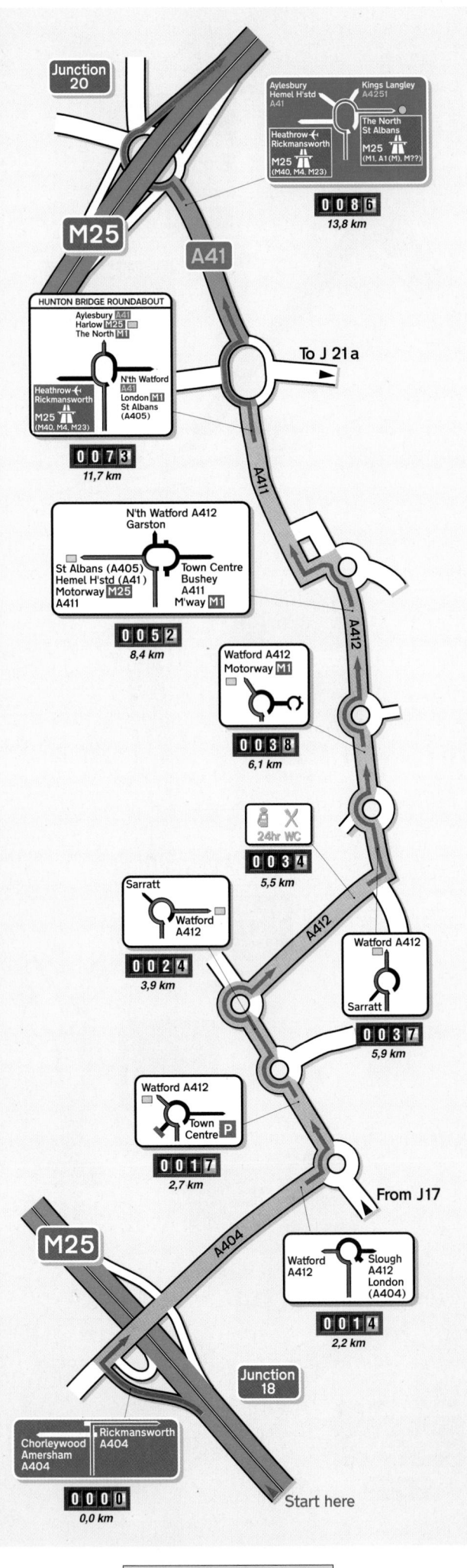

NOT TO SCALE

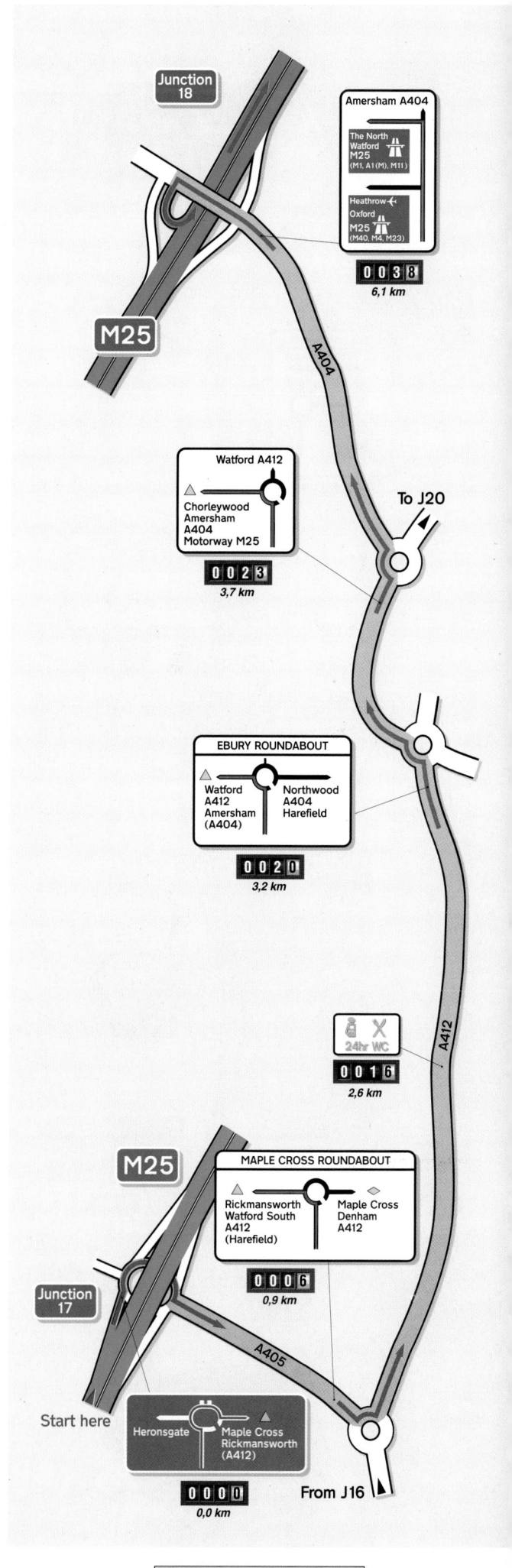

Junction 18

Amersham A404

The North
Watford
M25
(M1, A1(M), M11)

Heathrow
Oxford
M25
(M40, M4, M23)

0038
6,1 km

M25

A404

To J20

Watford A412

Chorleywood
Amersham
A404
Motorway M25

0023
3,7 km

EBURY ROUNDABOUT

Watford
A412
Amersham
(A404)

Northwood
A404
Harefield

0020
3,2 km

24hr WC

0016
2,6 km

A412

M25

MAPLE CROSS ROUNDABOUT

Rickmansworth
Watford South
A412
(Harefield)

Maple Cross
Denham
A412

0006
0,9 km

Junction 17

A405

Start here

Heronsgate
Rickmansworth
(A412)

Maple Cross

0000
0,0 km

From J16

NOT TO SCALE

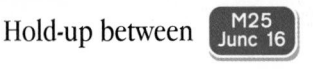 
Junction 17

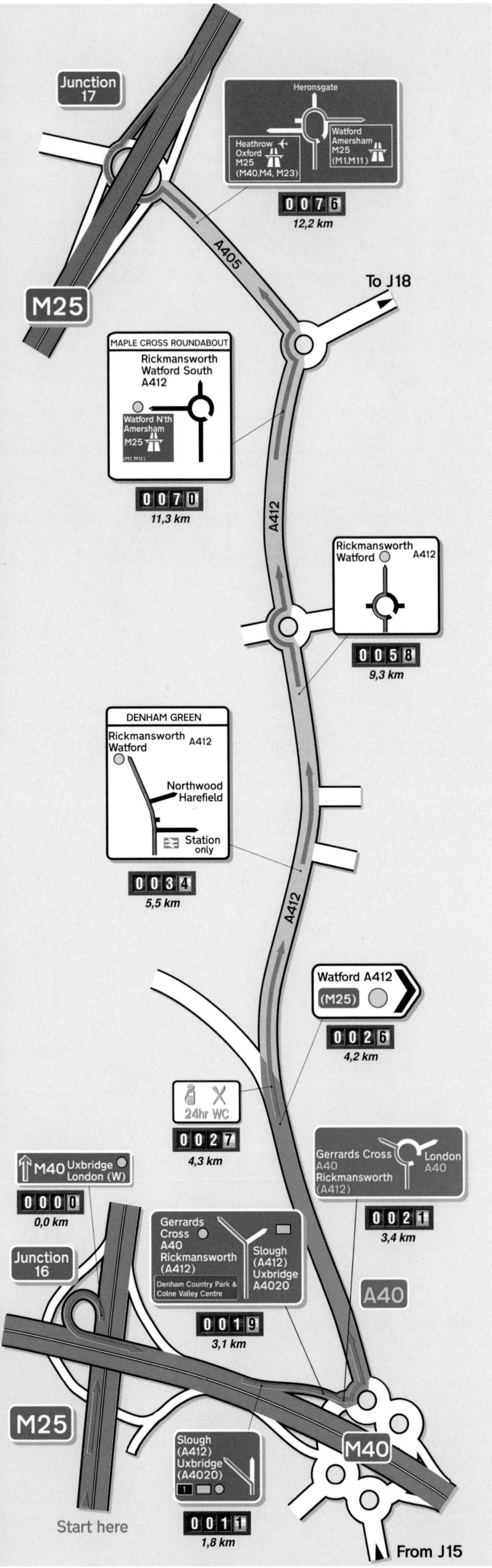

Heronsgate

Heathrow Oxford M25 (M40,M4, M23) | Watford Amersham M25 (M1,M11)

0 0 7 6
12,2 km

M25

To J18

A405

MAPLE CROSS ROUNDABOUT
Rickmansworth Watford South A412

Watford N'th Amersham M25 (M1,M11)

0 0 7 0
11,3 km

A412

Rickmansworth Watford A412

0 0 5 8
9,3 km

DENHAM GREEN
Rickmansworth Watford A412

Northwood Harefield

Station only

0 0 3 4
5,5 km

A412

Watford A412 (M25)

0 0 2 6
4,2 km

24hr WC

0 0 2 7
4,3 km

M40 Uxbridge London (W)

0 0 0 0
0,0 km

Gerrards Cross A40 Rickmansworth (A412) | London A40

0 0 2 1
3,4 km

Junction 16

Gerrards Cross A40 Rickmansworth (A412) | Slough (A412) Uxbridge A4020

Denham Country Park & Colne Valley Centre

0 0 1 9
3,1 km

M25

A40

M40

From J15

Slough (A412) Uxbridge (A4020)

0 0 1 1
1,8 km

Start here

NOT TO SCALE

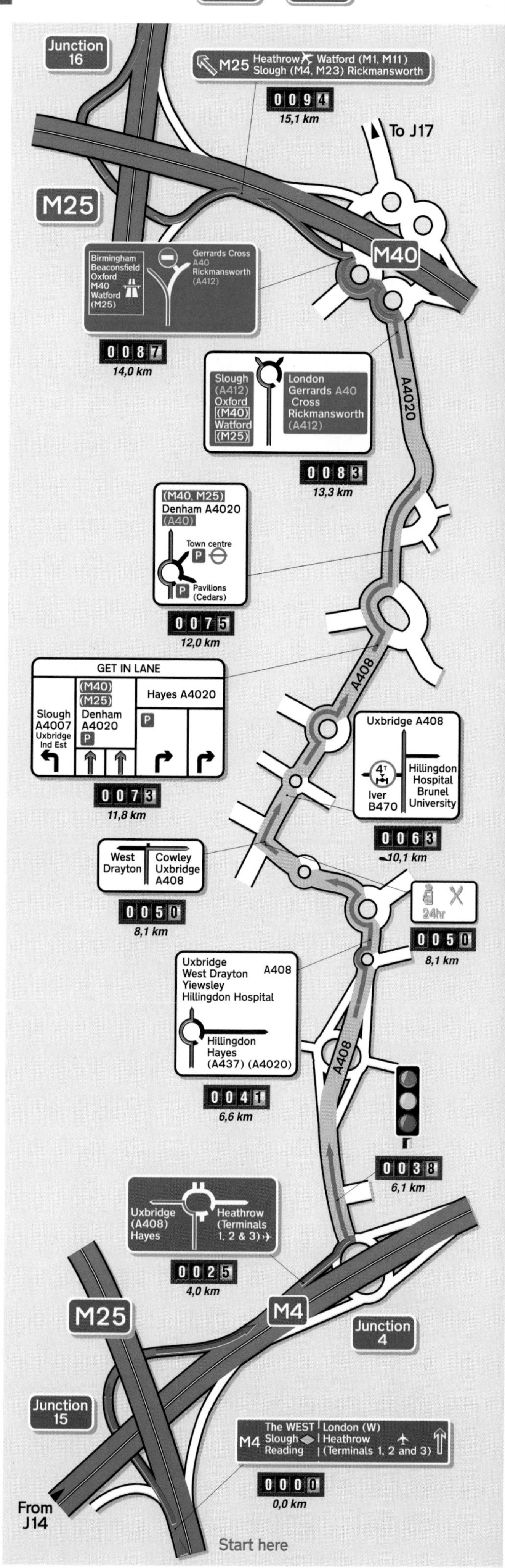

Junction 16

↰ M25 Heathrow ✈ Watford (M1, M11)
Slough (M4, M23) Rickmansworth

`0 0 9 4`
15,1 km

To J17

M25

M40

A4020

Birmingham
Beaconsfield
Oxford
M40 Watford
(M25)

Gerrards Cross
A40
Rickmansworth
(A412)

`0 0 8 7`
14,0 km

Slough
(A412)
Oxford
(M40)
Watford
(M25)

London
Gerrards A40
Cross
Rickmansworth
(A412)

`0 0 8 3`
13,3 km

(M40, M25)
Denham A4020
(A40)

Town centre
P ⊖
P Pavilions
(Cedars)

`0 0 7 5`
12,0 km

GET IN LANE

(M40)
(M25)

Slough
A4007
Uxbridge
Ind Est

Denham
A4020
P

Hayes A4020

P

`0 0 7 3`
11,8 km

A4408

Uxbridge A408

4ᵀ
Iver
B470

Hillingdon
Hospital
Brunel
University

`0 0 6 3`
—10,1 km

West
Drayton

Cowley
Uxbridge
A408

`0 0 5 0`
8,1 km

🧴 ✕
24hr

`0 0 5 0`
8,1 km

Uxbridge
West Drayton
Yiewsley
Hillingdon Hospital

A408

Hillingdon
Hayes
(A437) (A4020)

`0 0 4 1`
6,6 km

A408

`0 0 3 8`
6,1 km

Uxbridge
(A408)
Hayes

Heathrow
(Terminals
1, 2 & 3) ✈

`0 0 2 5`
4,0 km

M25

M4

Junction 4

Junction 15

The WEST
Slough ◆
Reading

London (W)
Heathrow
(Terminals 1, 2 and 3) ✈

M4

⬆

`0 0 0 0`
0,0 km

From J14

Start here

NOT TO SCALE

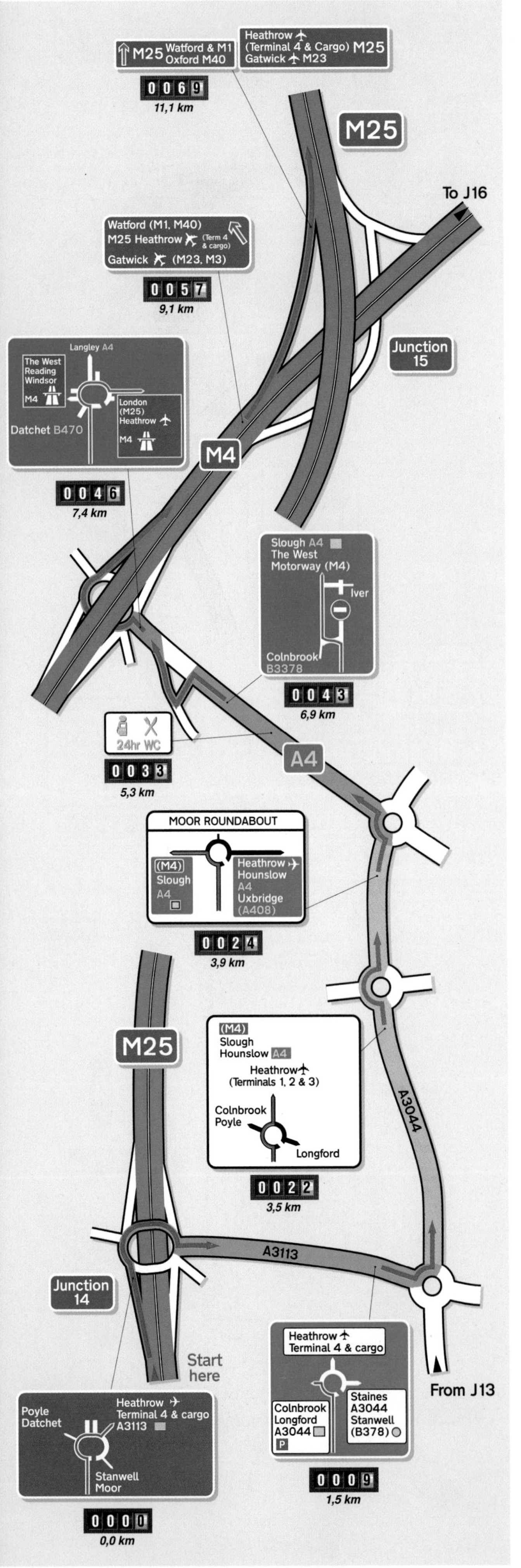

↑↑ M25 Watford & M1
Oxford M40
0 0 6 9
11,1 km

Heathrow ✈
(Terminal 4 & Cargo) **M25**
Gatwick ✈ M23

M25

To J16

Watford (M1, M40)
M25 Heathrow ✈ (Term 4 & cargo)
Gatwick ✈ (M23, M3)
0 0 5 7
9,1 km

Junction 15

Langley A4
The West
Reading
Windsor
M4
London
(M25)
Heathrow ✈
M4
Datchet B470
0 0 4 6
7,4 km

M4

Slough A4 ■
The West
Motorway (M4)
Iver
Colnbrook
B3378
0 0 4 3
6,9 km

🛏 ✕ 24hr WC
0 0 3 3
5,3 km

A4

MOOR ROUNDABOUT
(M4)
Slough
A4 ■
Heathrow ✈
Hounslow
A4
Uxbridge
(A408)
0 0 2 4
3,9 km

M25

(M4)
Slough
Hounslow A4
Heathrow ✈
(Terminals 1, 2 & 3)
Colnbrook
Poyle
Longford
0 0 2 2
3,5 km

A3044

A3113

Junction 14

Start
here

Heathrow ✈
Terminal 4 & cargo

Colnbrook
Longford
A3044 ■
P

Staines
A3044
Stanwell
(B378) ◎

From J13

0 0 0 9
1,5 km

Poyle
Datchet
Heathrow ✈
Terminal 4 & cargo
A3113 ■
Stanwell
Moor
0 0 0 0
0,0 km

NOT TO SCALE

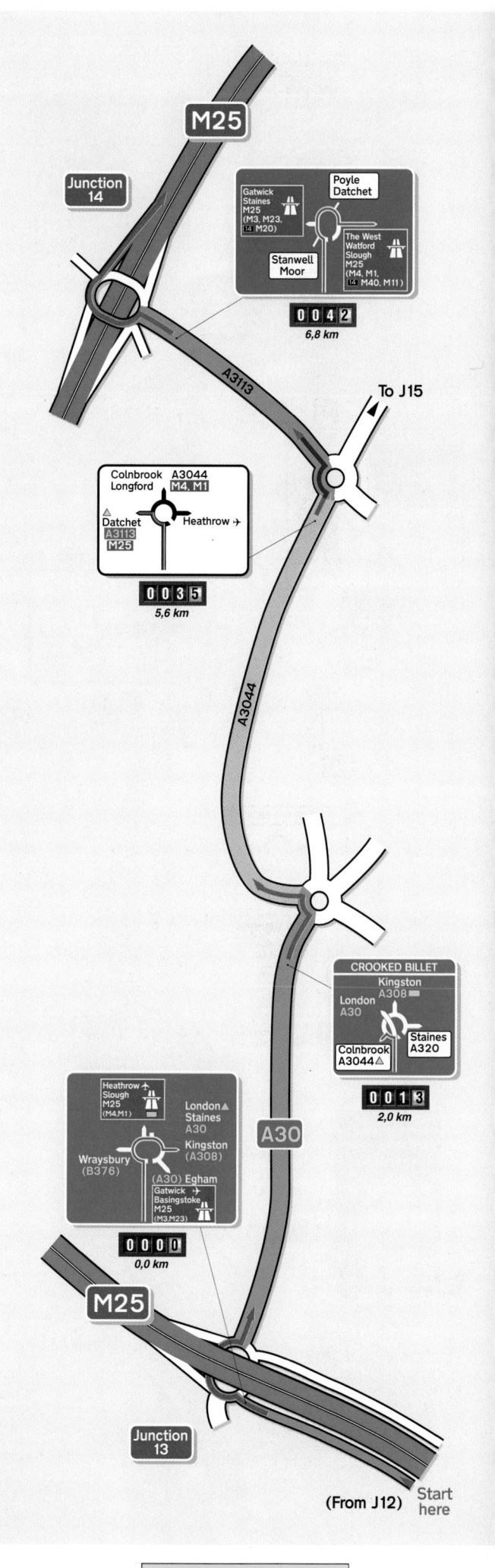

NOT TO SCALE

Hold-up between M3 Junc 3 M25 Junc 13 Clockwise

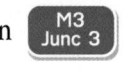

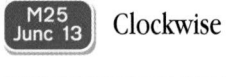

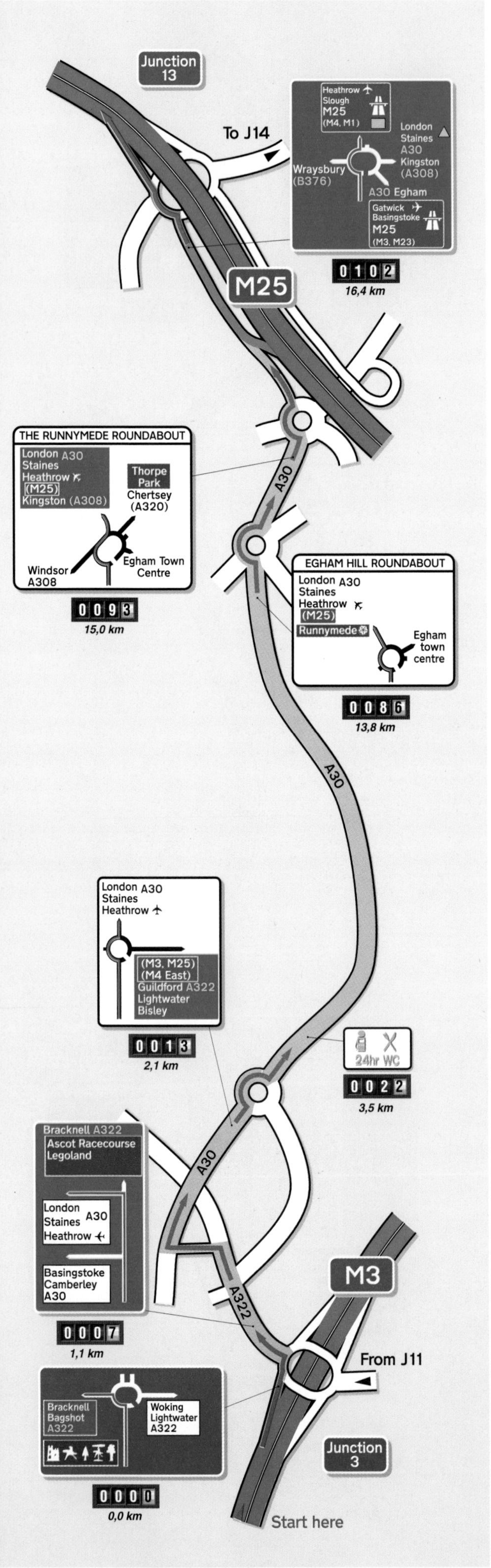

NOT TO SCALE

Junction 3

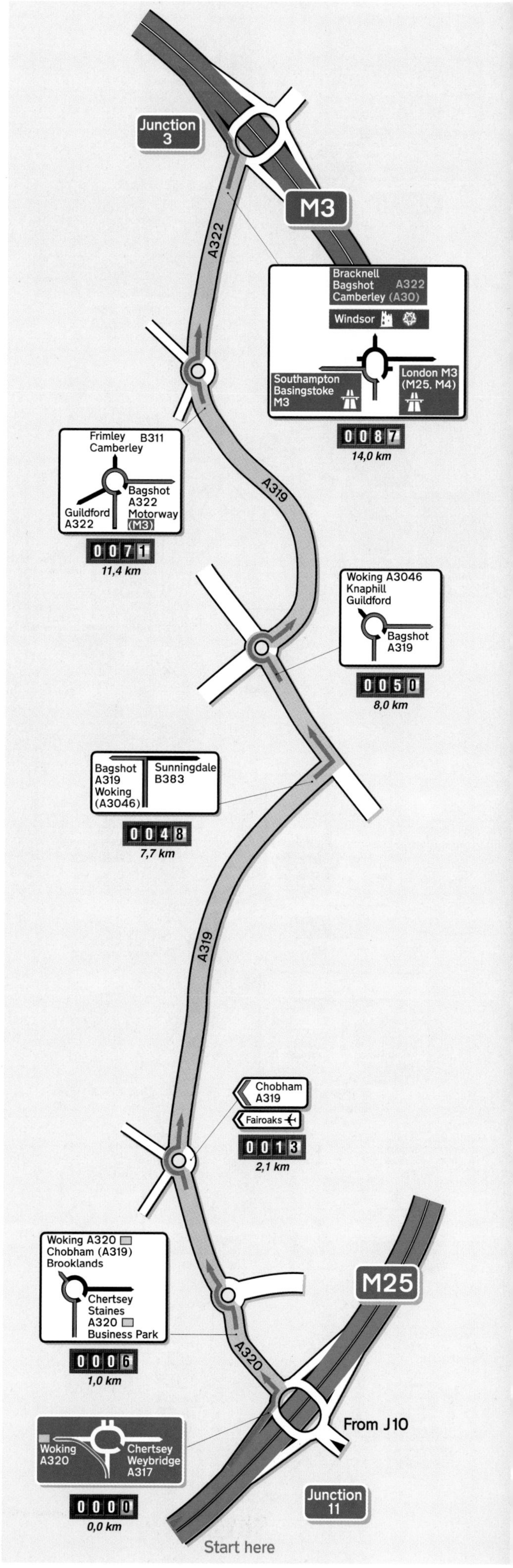

M3

Bracknell
Bagshot A322
Camberley (A30)

Windsor

Southampton   London M3
Basingstoke   (M25, M4)
M3

`0 0 8 7`
14,0 km

A322

A319

Frimley   B311
Camberley

Bagshot
A322
Guildford   Motorway
A322   (M3)

`0 0 7 1`
11,4 km

Woking A3046
Knaphill
Guildford

Bagshot
A319

`0 0 5 0`
8,0 km

Bagshot   Sunningdale
A319   B383
Woking
(A3046)

`0 0 4 8`
7,7 km

A319

Chobham
A319

Fairoaks

`0 0 1 3`
2,1 km

M25

Woking A320
Chobham (A319)
Brooklands

Chertsey
Staines
A320
Business Park

`0 0 0 6`
1,0 km

A320

From J10

Woking   Chertsey
A320   Weybridge
              A317

`0 0 0 0`
0,0 km

Junction
11

Start here

NOT TO SCALE

Heathrow
Slough
M25
(M4, M1)

London
Staines
A30
Kingston
(A308)

Wraysbury
(B376)

A30 Egham

Gatwick
Basingstoke
M25
(M3, M23)

0 0 7 4
12,0 km

Junction 13

Heathrow
Slough
M25
(M4, M1, M11)

Wraysbury
(B376)

London (W)
Staines A30

Gatwick
Basingstoke
M25
(M3, M23, M20)

0 0 7 3
11,7 km

M25

R Thames

A308

To J14

Windsor
A308

(M25)

Egham
Town

Chertsey
(A320)

Thorpe Park

0 0 6 9
11,2 km

Egham
Windsor
(A30)
M25 (M3)

Thorpe
B376
Chertsey
Woking
Thorpe Pk

Staines
Town
Centre
Wraysbury
(B376)

A320

0 0 5 7
9,1 km

0 0 4 2
6,8 km

Thorpe B388
V. Water (B389)
Staines
Avoiding Low Bridge

St Ann's Hill
Lyne

Staines
A320
Thorpe Park

0 0 2 6
4,2 km

Staines A320

Thorpe
Park

Penton
Marina

0 0 3 7
6,0 km

M3

Staines
A320

Thorpe
Virginia Water

Thorpe Park

Weybridge
Addlestone
A317
Town
Centre
Station

A320

0 0 2 2
3,5 km

St Peter's
Hospital
H
A&E

Chertsey
Staines
A320

Thorpe Park

M.O.D
Chertsey

Hillswood
Business Park

0 0 0 9
1,4 km

Staines A320
Town
Centre

0 0 2 0
3,2 km

M25

Woking A320
Chobham (A319)
Brooklands

Chertsey
Staines
A320
Business Park

0 0 0 5
0,9 km

From J10

Junction 11

Woking
A320

Chertsey
Weybridge
A317

A320

0 0 0 0
0,0 km

Start here

NOT TO SCALE   HGV
WARNING! 13'-3"

Hold-up between M25 Junc 10 M25 Junc 11 Clockwise

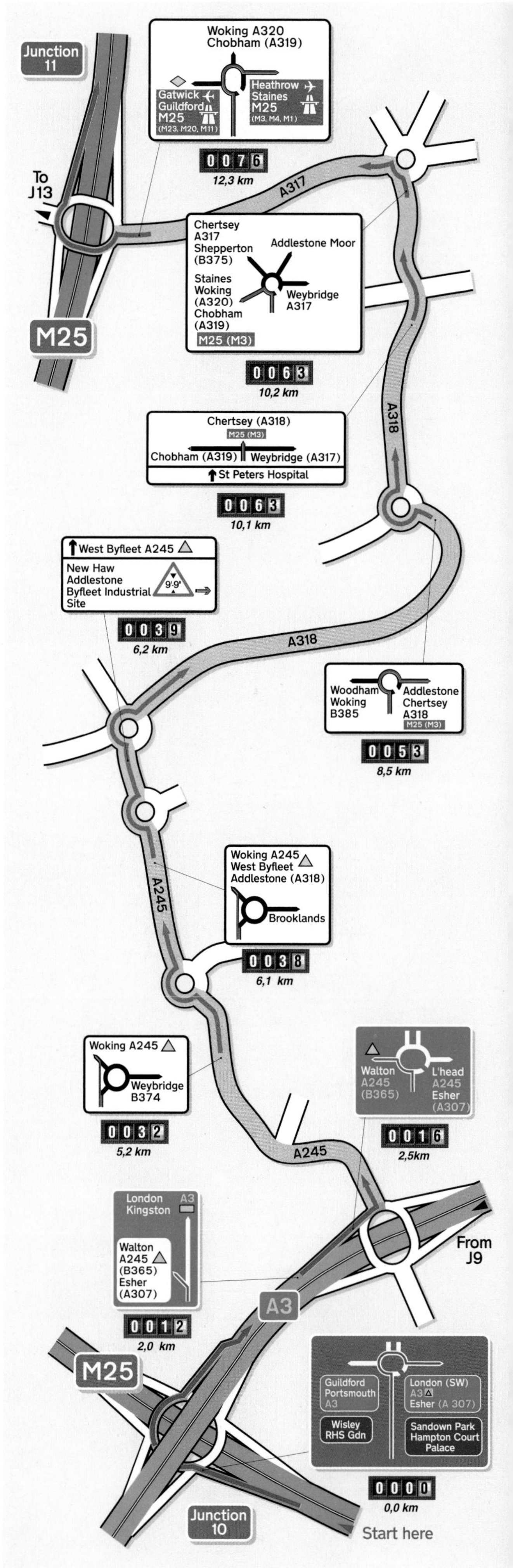
Junction 11
Woking A320
Chobham (A319)
Gatwick
Guildford
M25
(M23, M20, M11)
Heathrow
Staines
M25
(M3, M4, M1)
0076
12,3 km
To J13
A317
Chertsey
A317
Shepperton
(B375)
Staines
Woking
(A320)
Chobham
(A319)
M25 (M3)
Addlestone Moor
Weybridge
A317
M25
0063
10,2 km
A318
Chertsey (A318)
M25 (M3)
Chobham (A319)
Weybridge (A317)
St Peters Hospital
0063
10,1 km
West Byfleet A245
New Haw
Addlestone
Byfleet Industrial
Site
9'9"
0039
6,2 km
A318
Woodham
Woking
B385
Addlestone
Chertsey
A318
M25 (M3)
0053
8,5 km
Woking A245
West Byfleet
Addlestone (A318)
Brooklands
A245
0038
6,1 km
Woking A245
Weybridge
B374
0032
5,2 km
Walton
A245
(B365)
L'head
A245
Esher
(A307)
0016
2,5km
A245
London
Kingston
A3
Walton
A245
(B365)
Esher
(A307)
From J9
A3
0012
2,0 km
M25
Guildford
Portsmouth
A3
London (SW)
A3
Esher (A 307)
Wisley
RHS Gdn
Sandown Park
Hampton Court
Palace
0000
0,0 km
Junction 10
Start here

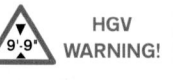

9'9" HGV WARNING!

NOT TO SCALE

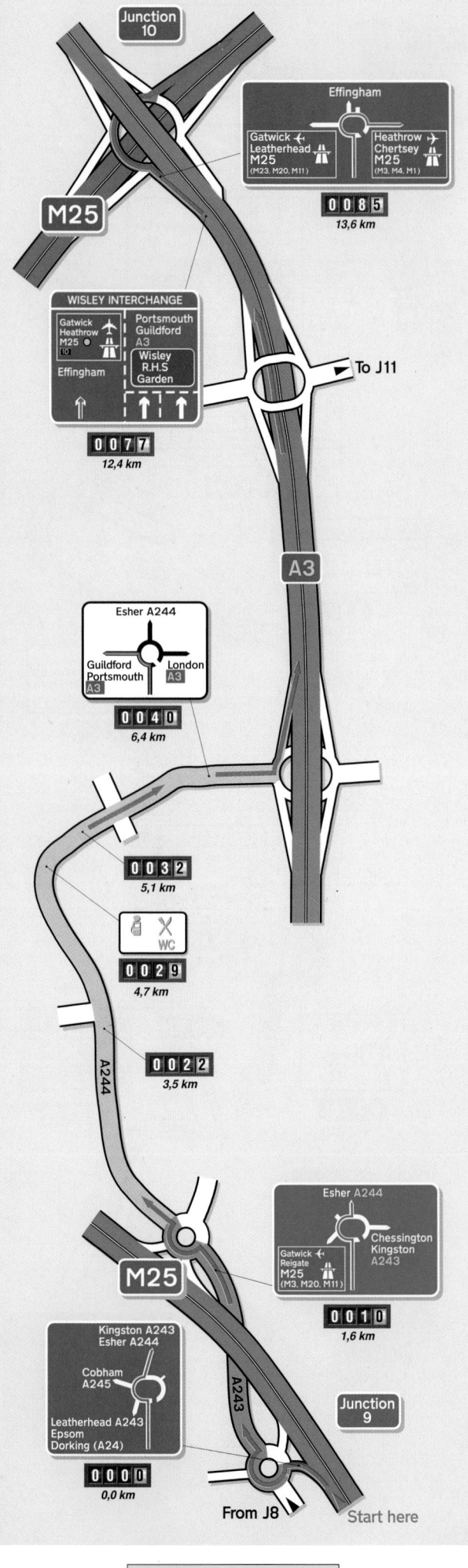

NOT TO SCALE

Hold-up between M25 Junc 8 M25 Junc 9 Clockwise

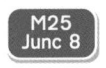

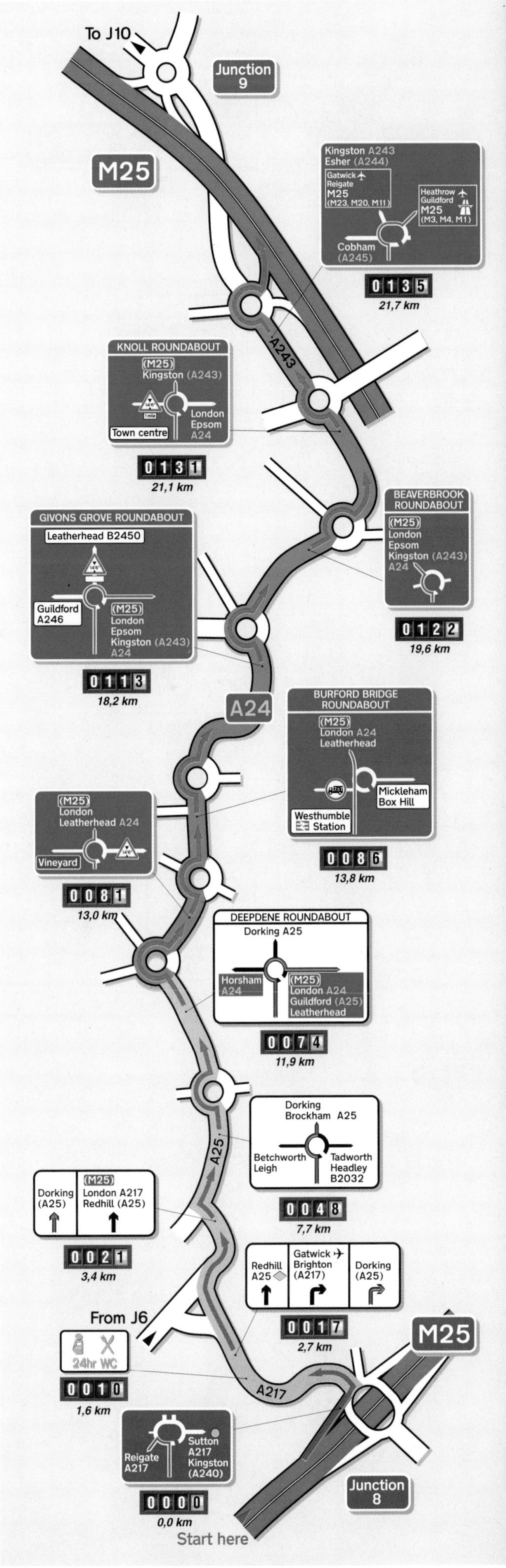
To J10
Junction 9
M25
Kingston A243
Esher (A244)
Gatwick
Reigate
M25
(M23, M20, M11)
Heathrow
Guildford
M25
(M3, M4, M1)
Cobham
(A245)
0135
21,7 km
A243
KNOLL ROUNDABOUT
(M25)
Kingston (A243)
London
Epsom
A24
Town centre
0131
21,1 km
BEAVERBROOK ROUNDABOUT
(M25)
London
Epsom
Kingston (A243)
A24
0122
19,6 km
GIVONS GROVE ROUNDABOUT
Leatherhead B2450
Guildford
A246
(M25)
London
Epsom
Kingston (A243)
A24
0113
18,2 km
A24
BURFORD BRIDGE ROUNDABOUT
(M25)
London A24
Leatherhead
Mickleham
Box Hill
Westhumble
Station
0086
13,8 km
(M25)
London
Leatherhead A24
Vineyard
0081
13,0 km
DEEPDENE ROUNDABOUT
Dorking A25
Horsham
A24
(M25)
London A24
Guildford (A25)
Leatherhead
0074
11,9 km
Dorking
Brockham A25
Betchworth
Leigh
Tadworth
Headley
B2032
0048
7,7 km
A25
Dorking
(A25)
(M25)
London A217
Redhill (A25)
0021
3,4 km
Redhill
A25
Gatwick
Brighton
(A217)
Dorking
(A25)
0017
2,7 km
From J6
24hr WC
0010
1,6 km
M25
A217
Reigate
A217
Sutton
A217
Kingston
(A240)
0000
0,0 km
Start here
Junction 8

NOT TO SCALE

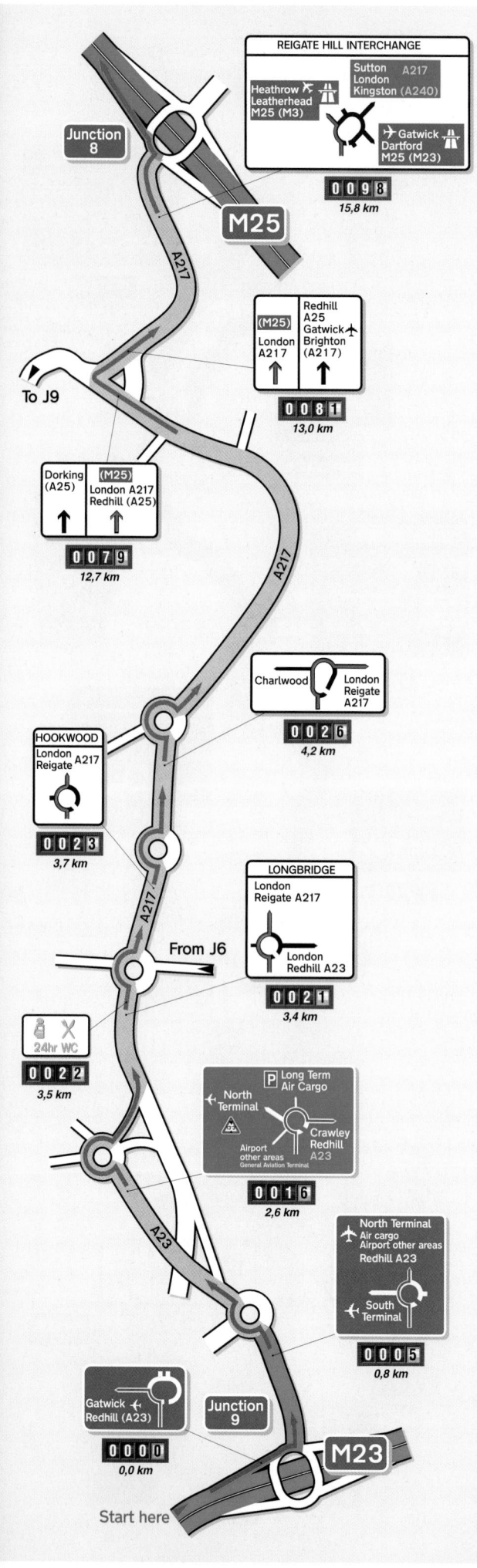

NOT TO SCALE

Hold-up between M25 Junc 6 – M23 Junc 9 Clockwise

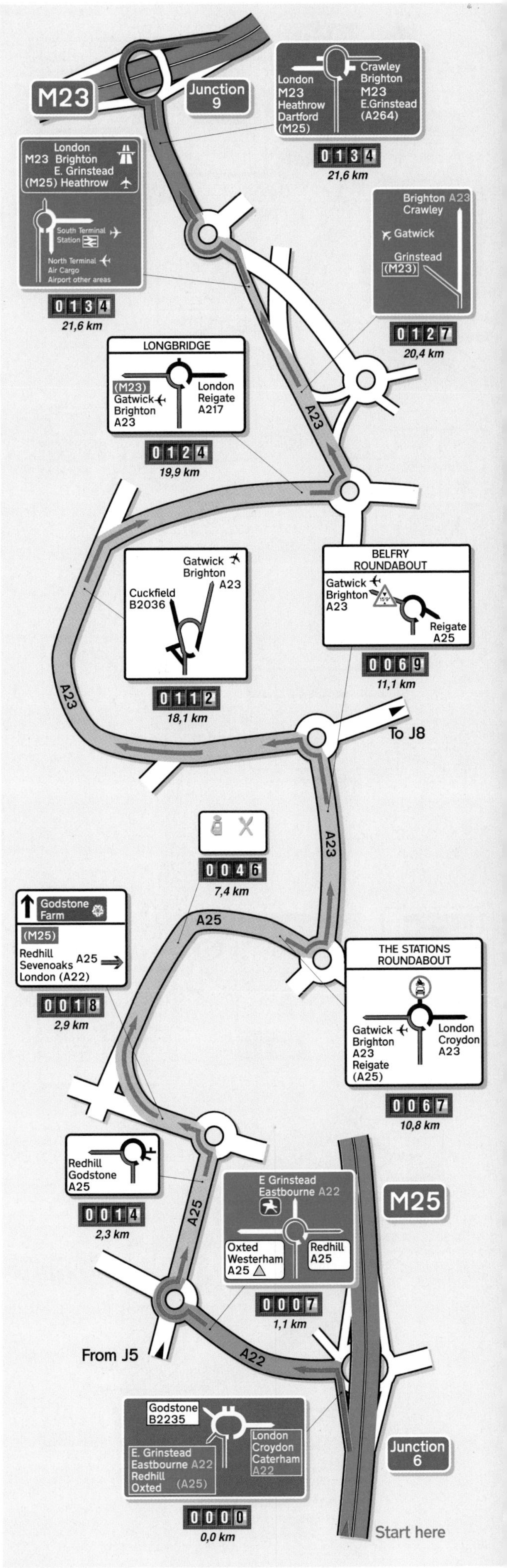
M23
Junction 9
London
M23
Heathrow
Dartford
(M25)
Crawley
Brighton
M23
E.Grinstead
(A264)
0134
21,6 km
London
M23 Brighton
E. Grinstead
(M25) Heathrow
South Terminal
Station
North Terminal
Air Cargo
Airport other areas
0134
21,6 km
Brighton A23
Crawley
Gatwick
Grinstead
(M23)
0127
20,4 km
LONGBRIDGE
(M23)
Gatwick
Brighton
A23
London
Reigate
A217
0124
19,9 km
A23
Gatwick
Brighton
A23
Cuckfield
B2036
0112
18,1 km
BELFRY
ROUNDABOUT
Gatwick
Brighton
A23
15'9"
Reigate
A25
0069
11,1 km
A23
To J8
A23
0046
7,4 km
Godstone
Farm
(M25)
Redhill
Sevenoaks
London (A22)
A25
0018
2,9 km
A25
THE STATIONS
ROUNDABOUT
Gatwick
Brighton
A23
Reigate
(A25)
London
Croydon
A23
0067
10,8 km
Redhill
Godstone
A25
0014
2,3 km
A25
E Grinstead
Eastbourne A22
Oxted
Westerham
A25
Redhill
A25
M25
0007
1,1 km
From J5
A22
Godstone
B2235
E. Grinstead
Eastbourne A22
Redhill
Oxted (A25)
London
Croydon
Caterham
A22
Junction 6
0000
0,0 km
Start here

15'9" HGV WARNING!

NOT TO SCALE

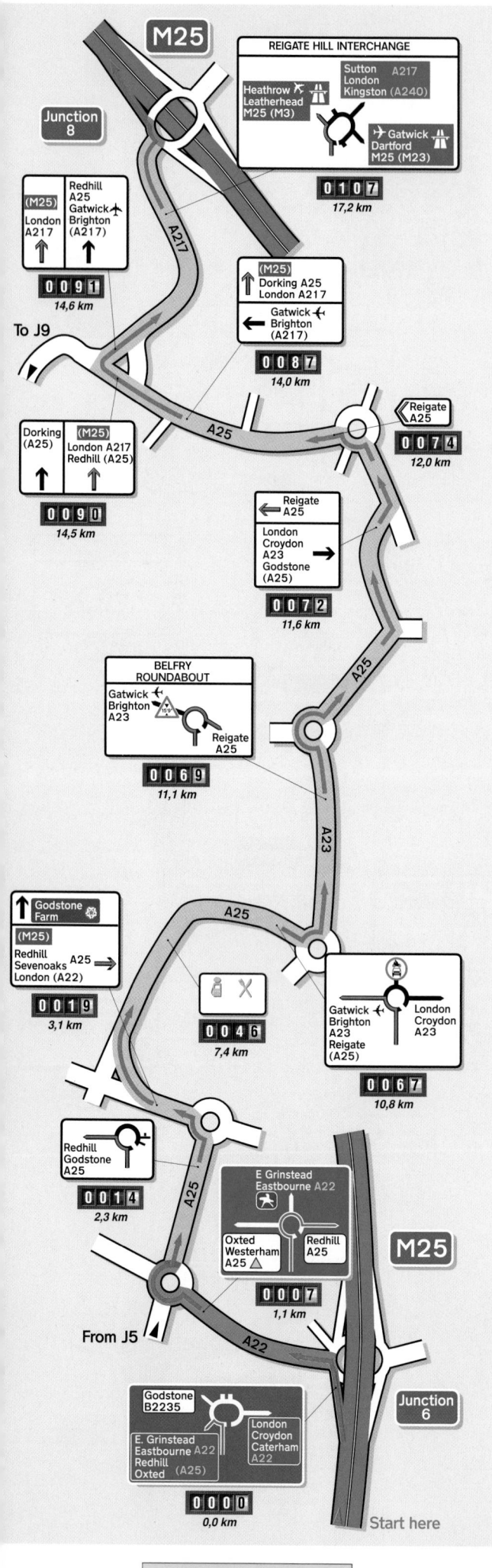

M25

REIGATE HILL INTERCHANGE

Sutton
London
Kingston (A240) A217

Heathrow
Leatherhead
M25 (M3)

✈ Gatwick
Dartford
M25 (M23)

`0 1 0 7`
17,2 km

Junction 8

Redhill
A25
Gatwick
Brighton
(A217)

(M25)
London
A217

`0 0 9 1`
14,6 km

A217

To J9

(M25)
Dorking A25
London A217

Gatwick ✈
Brighton
(A217)

`0 0 8 7`
14,0 km

A25

Reigate
A25

`0 0 7 4`
12,0 km

Dorking
(A25)

(M25)
London A217
Redhill (A25)

`0 0 9 0`
14,5 km

Reigate
A25

London
Croydon
A23
Godstone
(A25)

`0 0 7 2`
11,6 km

BELFRY ROUNDABOUT

Gatwick ✈
Brighton
A23   15,9

Reigate
A25

`0 0 6 9`
11,1 km

A25

A23

Godstone
Farm

(M25)
Redhill
Sevenoaks
London (A22) A25 →

`0 0 1 9`
3,1 km

A25

`0 0 4 6`
7,4 km

Gatwick
Brighton
A23
Reigate
(A25)

London
Croydon
A23

`0 0 6 7`
10,8 km

Redhill
Godstone
A25

`0 0 1 4`
2,3 km

A25

E Grinstead
Eastbourne A22

Oxted
Westerham
A25

Redhill
A25

`0 0 0 7`
1,1 km

M25

From J5

A22

Godstone
B2235

E. Grinstead
Eastbourne A22
Redhill
Oxted (A25)

London
Croydon
Caterham
A22

`0 0 0 0`
0,0 km

Junction 6

Start here

NOT TO SCALE

Hold-up between M25 Junc 5 M25 Junc 6 Clockwise

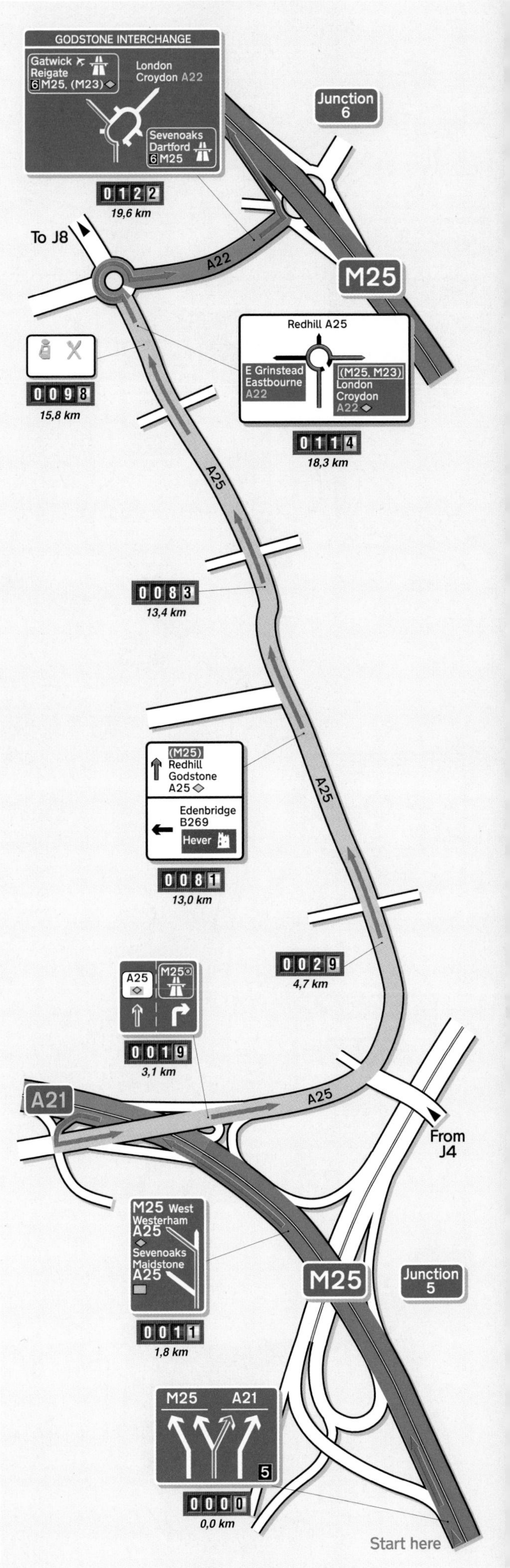
GODSTONE INTERCHANGE
Gatwick
Reigate
6 M25, (M23)
London
Croydon A22
Sevenoaks
Dartford
6 M25
0122
19,6 km
Junction 6
To J8
A22
M25
Redhill A25
E Grinstead
Eastbourne
A22
(M25, M23)
London
Croydon
A22
0114
18,3 km
0098
15,8 km
A25
0083
13,4 km
(M25)
Redhill
Godstone
A25
Edenbridge
B269
Hever
0081
13,0 km
A25
0029
4,7 km
A25
M25
0019
3,1 km
A21
A25
From J4
M25 West
Westerham
A25
Sevenoaks
Maidstone
A25
0011
1,8 km
M25
Junction 5
M25
A21
5
0000
0,0 km
Start here

NOT TO SCALE

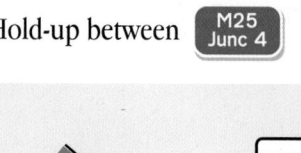
A21

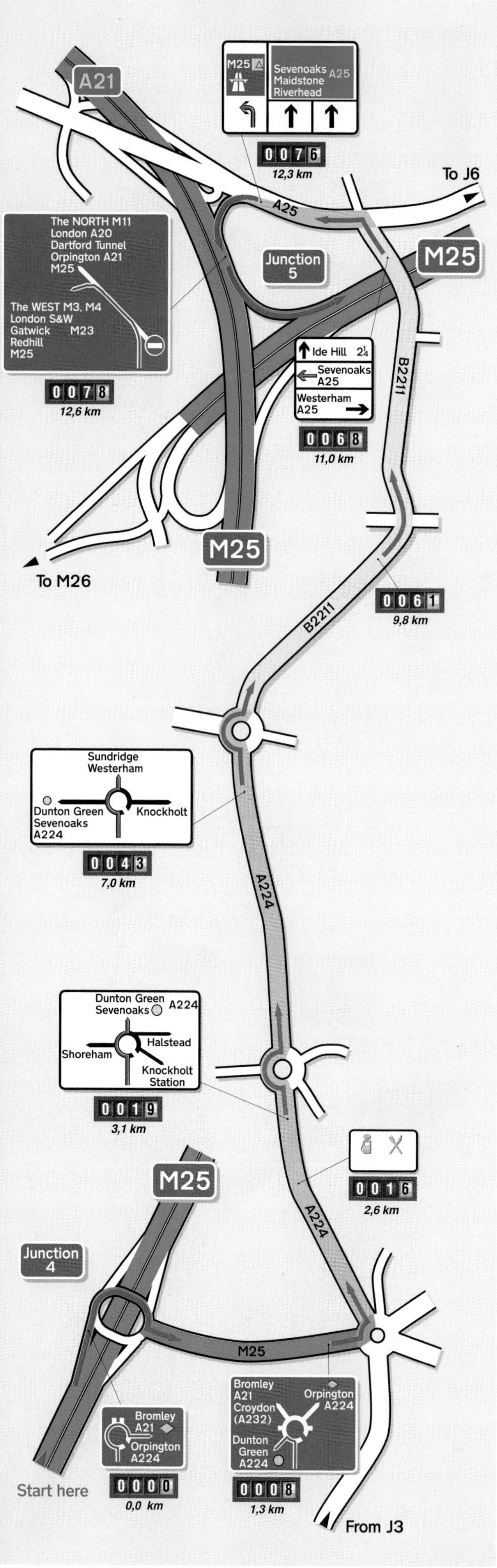

M25 🛆
Sevenoaks A25
Maidstone
Riverhead
← ↑ ↑
0 0 7 6
12,3 km

To J6

A25

Junction
5

M25

The NORTH M11
London A20
Dartford Tunnel
Orpington A21
M25

The WEST M3, M4
London S&W
Gatwick   M23
Redhill
M25

0 0 7 8
12,6 km

↑ Ide Hill   2¼
← Sevenoaks
A25
Westerham →
A25

0 0 6 8
11,0 km

B2211

M25

To M26

B2211

0 0 6 1
9,8 km

Sundridge
Westerham

Dunton Green   Knockholt
Sevenoaks
A224

0 0 4 3
7,0 km

A224

Dunton Green
Sevenoaks ○ A224

Shoreham   Halstead
Knockholt
Station

0 0 1 9
3,1 km

🍴 ✗
0 0 1 6
2,6 km

M25

A224

Junction
4

M25

Bromley
A21
Croydon   Orpington
(A232)   A224

Dunton
Green
A224

Bromley
A21 ◆
Orpington
A224

Start here   **0 0 0 0**
0,0 km

0 0 0 8
1,3 km

From J3

NOT TO SCALE

Hold-up between M25 Junc 3 M25 Junc 4 Clockwise

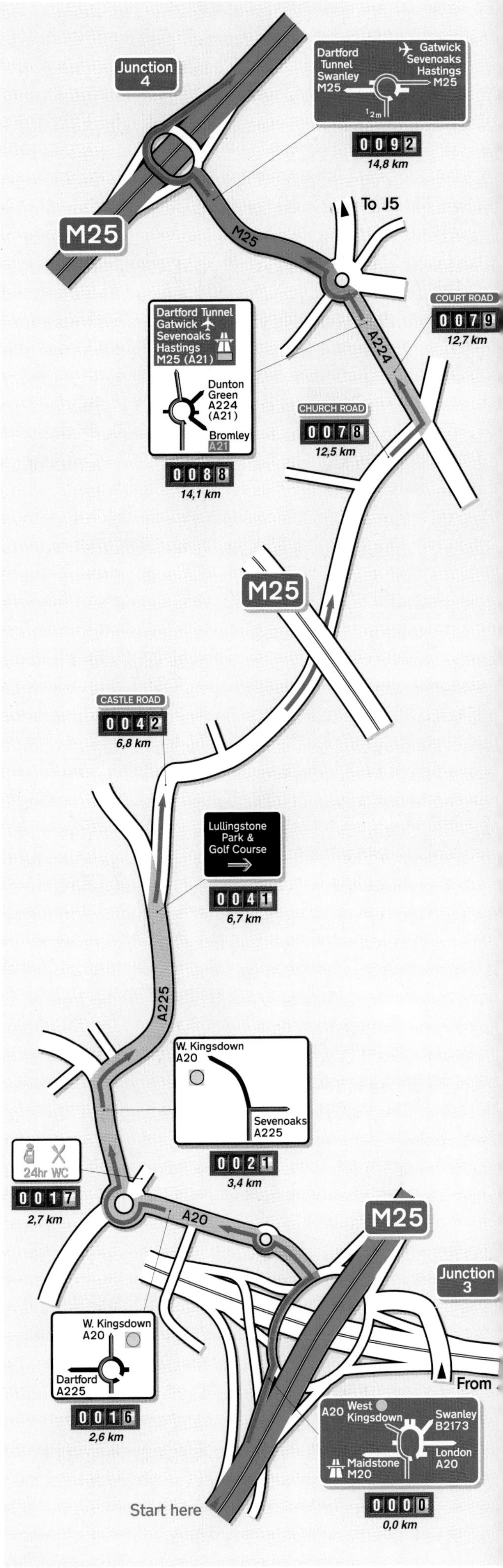
Junction 4
M25
Dartford Tunnel Swanley M25
Gatwick Sevenoaks Hastings M25
0092
14,8 km
To J5
M25
COURT ROAD
0079
12,7 km
A224
Dartford Tunnel
Gatwick
Sevenoaks
Hastings
M25 (A21)
Dunton Green A224 (A21)
Bromley A21
0088
14,1 km
CHURCH ROAD
0078
12,5 km
M25
CASTLE ROAD
0042
6,8 km
Lullingstone Park & Golf Course
0041
6,7 km
A225
W. Kingsdown A20
Sevenoaks A225
0021
3,4 km
24hr WC
0017
2,7 km
A20
M25
Junction 3
W. Kingsdown A20
Dartford A225
0016
2,6 km
From
A20 West Kingsdown
Swanley B2173
London A20
Maidstone M20
0000
0,0 km
Start here

HGV WARNING! **NOT TO SCALE**

W. Kingsdown A20

Gatwick
Sevenoaks
M25
(M23,M4)

Dartford
Tunnel
M25
(M11,M1)

Swanley
B2173

M20

To J4

M25

Junction
3

0 1 1 2
18,1 km

M25   M20
A20

1 m

0 0 9 9
15,9 km

A20

A223

Orpington (A224)
Croydon (A232)
Central
London (A20,A2)

Maidstone
Dover   A20   (M20)
Dartford Tunnel
Sevenoaks   (M25)

0 0 6 8
11,0 km

24hr

0 0 6 6
10,6 km

Foots Cray
avoiding weak bridge
Central London (A20, A2)
Orpington (A224)
Maidstone (A20) (M20)
Dover
Dartford Tunnel (M25)
Sevenoaks

Swanley
B2173   Foots Cray
A211

0 0 6 3
10,1 km

A2018

Bexley
avoiding weak bridge

Bexley
A223

Sidcup
(A211)
Orpington
(A224)

7.5T
mgw   15'0"

0 0 4 2
6,8 km

Bexley A2018
Sidcup (A223)

Wilmington

0 0 3 0
4,8 km

Dartford (W)
Crayford
A2018

2-3 m

0 0 2 1
3,4 km

Sidcup
Orpington
A2018   Dartford (W)
Crayford
A2018

0 0 2 9
4,7 km

A2

M25

Gatwick (M23) M25
Channel Tnl (M20)
Dover   London A2

0 0 0 1
0,1 km

Junction
2

M'Way (M2) A2   London
Canterbury   A2
Non Motorway Traffic

0 0 0 0
0,0 km

From
J1a   Start here

NOT TO SCALE

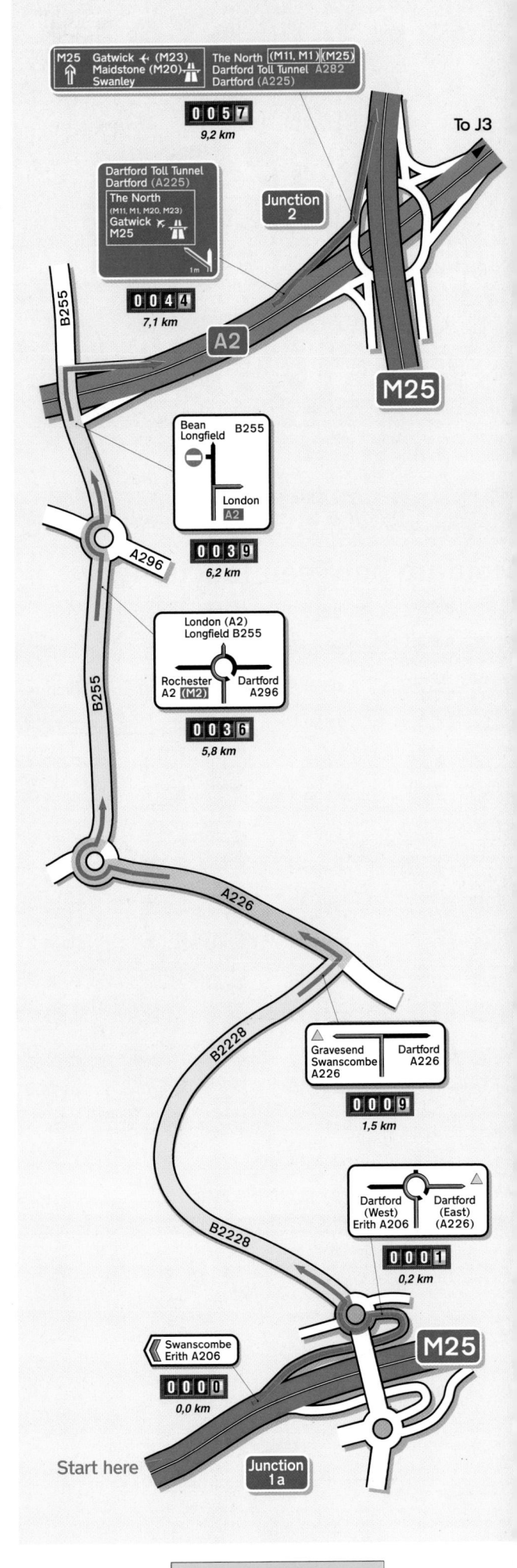

To J3

M25 Gatwick ← (M23) The North (M11, M1) (M25)
Maidstone (M20) Dartford Toll Tunnel A282
Swanley Dartford (A225)

0 0 5 7
9,2 km

Dartford Toll Tunnel
Dartford (A225)
The North
(M11, M1, M20, M23)
Gatwick ✈
M25
1 m

0 0 4 4
7,1 km

Junction 2

A2

M25

B255

Bean B255
Longfield
London
A2

0 0 3 9
6,2 km

A296

London (A2)
Longfield B255
Rochester Dartford
A2 ((M2)) A296

0 0 3 6
5,8 km

B255

A226

B2228

Gravesend Dartford
Swanscombe A226
A226

0 0 0 9
1,5 km

Dartford Dartford
(West) (East)
Erith A206 (A226)

0 0 0 1
0,2 km

B2228

M25

Swanscombe
Erith A206

0 0 0 0
0,0 km

Start here

Junction 1a

NOT TO SCALE

COLLINS

LONDON
M25
'jambuster' TM
GUIDE

CLOCKWISE

CONTENTS

Hold-up between Junctions:

First published by Give Way Ltd 1997
This revised edition published by Collins 1998
An *imprint of* HarperCollins*Publishers*
77-85 Fulham Palace Road, Hammersmith, London W6 8JB

Mapping pages 2 to 32 © Give Way Ltd, 1998
Mapping pages 33 © Bartholomew 1998

'jambuster' ™ Guides are designed and researched by Give Way Ltd, Newcastle upon Tyne.
Project Director - Neil Atkinson. Senior Designer - Matthew Cook.

'jambuster' ™ is a trademark of HarperCollins*Publishers*.

ISBN 0 0044 8846 6   LC9983 MNA